Education: A Very Short Introduction

VERY SHORT INTRODUCTIONS are for anyone wanting a stimulating and accessible way in to a new subject. They are written by experts and have been translated into more than 40 different languages. The series began in 1995 and now covers a wide variety of topics in every discipline. The VSI library contains nearly 400 volumes—a Very Short Introduction to everything from Indian philosophy to psychology and American history—and continues to grow in every subject area.

Very Short Introductions available now:

ACCOUNTING Christopher Nobes
ADVERTISING Winston Fletcher
AFRICAN HISTORY John Parker and
    Richard Rathbone
AGNOSTICISM Robin Le Poidevin
ALEXANDER THE GREAT
    Hugh Bowden
AMERICAN HISTORY Paul S. Boyer
AMERICAN IMMIGRATION
    David A. Gerber
AMERICAN POLITICAL PARTIES
    AND ELECTIONS L. Sandy Maisel
AMERICAN POLITICS Richard M. Valelly
THE AMERICAN PRESIDENCY
    Charles O. Jones
ANAESTHESIA Aidan O'Donnell
ANARCHISM Colin Ward
ANCIENT EGYPT Ian Shaw
ANCIENT GREECE Paul Cartledge
THE ANCIENT NEAR EAST
    Amanda H. Podany
ANCIENT PHILOSOPHY Julia Annas
ANCIENT WARFARE Harry Sidebottom
ANGELS David Albert Jones
ANGLICANISM Mark Chapman
THE ANGLO-SAXON AGE John Blair
THE ANIMAL KINGDOM Peter Holland
ANIMAL RIGHTS David DeGrazia
THE ANTARCTIC Klaus Dodds
ANTISEMITISM Steven Beller
ANXIETY Daniel Freeman and
    Jason Freeman
THE APOCRYPHAL GOSPELS
    Paul Foster
ARCHAEOLOGY Paul Bahn

ARCHITECTURE Andrew Ballantyne
ARISTOCRACY William Doyle
ARISTOTLE Jonathan Barnes
ART HISTORY Dana Arnold
ART THEORY Cynthia Freeland
ASTROBIOLOGY David C. Catling
ATHEISM Julian Baggini
AUGUSTINE Henry Chadwick
AUSTRALIA Kenneth Morgan
AUTISM Uta Frith
THE AVANT GARDE David Cottington
THE AZTECS David Carrasco
BACTERIA Sebastian G. B. Amyes
BARTHES Jonathan Culler
THE BEATS David Sterritt
BEAUTY Roger Scruton
BESTSELLERS John Sutherland
THE BIBLE John Riches
BIBLICAL ARCHAEOLOGY Eric H. Cline
BIOGRAPHY Hermione Lee
THE BLUES Elijah Wald
THE BOOK OF MORMON Terryl Givens
BORDERS Alexander C. Diener and
    Joshua Hagen
THE BRAIN Michael O'Shea
THE BRITISH CONSTITUTION
    Martin Loughlin
THE BRITISH EMPIRE Ashley Jackson
BRITISH POLITICS Anthony Wright
BUDDHA Michael Carrithers
BUDDHISM Damien Keown
BUDDHIST ETHICS Damien Keown
CANCER Nicholas James
CAPITALISM James Fulcher
CATHOLICISM Gerald O'Collins

Gary Thomas

EDUCATION

A Very Short Introduction

OXFORD
UNIVERSITY PRESS

OXFORD
UNIVERSITY PRESS

Great Clarendon Street, Oxford, OX2 6DP,
United Kingdom

Oxford University Press is a department of the University of Oxford.
It furthers the University's objective of excellence in research, scholarship,
and education by publishing worldwide. Oxford is a registered trade mark of
Oxford University Press in the UK and in certain other countries

First Edition published in 2013

Impression: 4

British Library Cataloguing in Publication Data
Data available

ISBN 978-0-19-964326-4

Printed in Great Britain by
Ashford Colour Press Ltd, Gosport, Hampshire

Contents

Preface

Few people know very much about why schools exist as they do today; the intellectual traditions that have shaped education seem to be invisible to most observers. This is a strange gap in the knowledge of the public. With physics, most informed laypeople could write a coherent sentence or two about Einstein and Newton. For biology, a page might be forthcoming on Darwin. Even for economics most could probably say something sensible about Keynes and Marx. But for education, most, I think, would struggle to offer anything at all about Dewey or Piaget. It is perhaps this gap in awareness and understanding about what education is and how it has developed that has contributed to the dearth of creativity about how to improve it.

Maybe this gap in knowledge says something about the way we view education in the West. It's telling, for example, that when the American philosopher John Dewey—arguably the greatest thinker about education in modern times—visited China in 1928 to collect an honorary degree from the National University at Peking, its rector hailed him as 'the second Confucius'. I don't think this was hyperbole, and nor was it a joke: this was in China, after all, and comparisons with Confucius in China are surely made judiciously. There could be no greater praise for Dewey.

But, rued the editorial writer of *Time* magazine at the time, 'Not one American in ten thousand has ever heard of John Dewey.' Indeed, it's probably much the same today (and, no, he's not the Dewey who invented the library cataloguing system). Many Westerners seem to feel that compulsory attendance at school for ten years tells them all they need (or want) to know about education. Indeed, when John Major (the UK prime minister between 1990 and 1997) famously said that children needed to be studying education more assiduously at school, he gave the game away—'education' was, for him, simply a synonym for all the stuff you're expected to learn at school. Nothing more.

This isn't just a *short* introduction, it's a *very* short introduction and as such it's going to be prone to oversimplification, shallowness, omissions, and banality. How should I avoid these, I wondered, as I sat down to write. It was an especially tough question, given the breadth of education as a subject. I realized that I couldn't cover everything—at least not in a way that would avoid oversimplification. So, I've sacrificed comprehensiveness for discussion, and I've focused on ideas rather than facts.

Having made a decision about focus, and having a picture in my mind of *Very Short Introduction* readers as intelligent, well-informed people who may not have any special background in the subject about which they are reading, I've decided to try to tell a story, or a series of stories, about the ways that ideas about education have become shaped. Often the stories are intertwined, so there isn't a simple, clean narrative about, for example, progressive education: the story of its development is infused with the growth of psychology, of testing, of the findings of research about its consequences.

My views about education are refracted through my own trials and tribulations in schools. When I failed my 11-plus examination my parents in their wisdom sent me to a cheap (in every sense of the word) private school, which was like a modern Dotheboys Hall.

Here, in one lesson, I was caned twenty-three times (this was in 1966) by the English teacher, nicknamed 'Bonzo', whose cane was called, after the ice cream popular at the time, 'Mr Whippy'. Bonzo would always add the rider, 'Makes you scream, not ice cream,' notionally for comic effect, after calling a pupil for Mr Whippy's attention. When the school mercifully went bankrupt, I was sent to the local secondary modern school and then when I had proved myself by passing enough exams I was allowed to go to the grammar school and then university.

After university, I worked as a primary school teacher, an educational psychologist, and an academic in five universities. I have visited in my professional career two or three hundred schools, worked for five local authorities and I was a parent governor at the state comprehensive school attended by my own children. I was the termly taxi service for my daughters as they attended their two universities. I can honestly say, to quote Joni Mitchell, that I've looked at schools 'from both sides now', and in this book I include my personal views where this seems appropriate.

I'd like to thank both of my daughters for their help with the book—Kate, for helping with the diagrams, and Emily, who is a teacher in a comprehensive school, for her insightful comments on a draft. I am enormously grateful also to the anonymous UK and American readers of the book, who made invaluable comments, were hugely supportive and encouraged me to write something with more of my own opinions in it. Thanks to my colleagues at the University of Birmingham School of Education for their advice and ideas, though any errors of fact or judgement are entirely down to me.

List of Illustrations

Education

Chapter 1
Beginnings

Estimates for how long *Homo sapiens* has been on the planet range from 30,000 years to 200,000 years. No one is quite sure exactly how long. What is certain, though, is that the brains of our ancestor *Homo sapiens* were the same as our brains. We are the same people, physically: today, we have no additional neurons, no better wiring. But our tools for thinking—our ideas, hypotheses, theories, models—are marvellously improved. How to draw, how to write, how to think, have all been learned, sometimes with great difficulty, and the learning has been passed on. The only reason we are better at thinking and doing things now—the only reason that Aristotle, Michelangelo, and Einstein blazed into the intellectual firmament in the last couple of thousand years and not 30,000 years ago—is that we accumulate knowledge and pass ideas and information from one generation to the next. With the accumulation, we get better. And better.

The progress trajectory of *Homo sapiens* veers upward ever more steeply not just because of our cleverness but because of the ability of our species to crystallize and store knowledge in specialized sounds and language, and then play with it—build and forge and mould it and model with it—using it to grip hold of the past and to imagine and plan the future. But the really clever bit is that we can share it and build on it; we can pass all of this on to our offspring, friends, and colleagues. Out of our cleverness has emerged something almost more important than the cleverness itself. Out of it has come learning about how to share ideas and pass down skills and knowledge. Out of it has come education.

Education happens in myriad forms of communication: parents explaining ideas to their children; friends talking and sharing ideas; people demonstrating skills to each other; skilled craftsfolk apprenticing new colleagues to a trade; teachers teaching young people in schools and colleges. It happens all through life: in the immortal words of Riff in *West Side Story,* it's womb to tomb. It's all education. And we should, emphatically, remember that education isn't just about what happens in schools and colleges. This book is mostly about schools and what goes on in them, for schools are the specialized institutions that we have built, notionally, for the purpose of education. But we should remember that educators have fought through the ages to make school more about education, for the two phenomena, schools and education, are not, sadly, necessarily linked at all.

In fact, most famous quotations about education point to the putative connection between education and schools and are distinctly rude about the latter. For example, Mark Twain quipped, 'I have never let my schooling interfere with my education.' That's similar to Winston Churchill's 'The only time my education was interrupted was while I was at school.' And Albert Einstein asserted that 'Education is what remains when we have forgotten everything that has been learned at school.' Their message? Schools aren't necessary for education; in fact, they may get in the way of it.

How did we get to a point where many of the finest minds (along with even more not-so-fine minds) resent the time they spent at school? How did we arrive at a position where education and schooling are, for many, so far apart? It's worth remembering that the Latin root of the word 'education' is in *educere,* translating to something close to 'bringing out'—to a cultivation, a nurturing, of inner talents and skills. How did the activity of schools become so distanced from this? To try and throw some light on these questions I'll begin with a brief look at the growth of schools and at some of the questions that have accompanied that growth.

Schools and education

Detailed knowledge about the way schools first operated and our first evidence about the ways that people thought about education come from ancient Greece, in the 5th to 4th centuries BC. In fact, the word 'school' comes from the Greek *schole* and interestingly *schole* means leisure, giving a clue about how far ideas about education have changed between then and now. Then, it seems, the assumption was that leisure was synonymous with learning and contemplation. The Greeks had elementary schools for the teaching of reading and arithmetic, and they had ephebic colleges— secondary schools to us—with end-of-term examinations in geometry, grammar, music, and rhetoric. This looks quite familiar.

1. **Gustav Adolph Spangenberg's** *Aristotle's School*, **a representation of the Lyceum**

They also had their gymnasiums, such as Plato's Academy and Aristotle's Lyceum, where young men (only men) would train naked for public games. Alongside the naked sport, there was teaching, discussion, and research. Add clothes, and we can surely see the beginnings of the modern university here.

Plato dreamed of an ideal state in *The Republic* and he had much to say about that state's education. Anticipating the thoughts of progressive educators who would come two millennia later, Plato said (putting his case in the form of a Socratic dialogue, as was his wont):

> 'Now, all this study of reckoning and geometry and all the preliminary studies that are indispensable preparation for dialectics must be presented to them while still young, not in the form of compulsory instruction.' 'Why so?' 'Because,' said I, 'a free soul ought not to pursue any study slavishly; for while bodily labours performed under constraint do not harm the body, nothing that is learned under compulsion stays with the mind.' 'True,' he said. 'Do not, then, my friend, keep children to their studies by compulsion but by play.'
>
> *The Republic*, 536d–e; 537a

Plato flags up a tension here that remains recognizable to this day and which is at the core of much that I shall discuss in this book. It is between two divergent lines of thought about education: should we be telling children facts and ideas and telling them to learn them, or should we be encouraging them to discover knowledge for themselves?

Plato perhaps offered his commentary not only as a counterweight to what seems to have been a didactic bent developing in the ancient Greek curriculum but also in response to a certain brutality in its disciplinary methods, if one of the stories of the time in the *Mimes of Herodas* is anything to go by. In this story, *The Schoolmaster*, a mother brings her errant son to the teacher, complaining about his waywardness and indolence. She asks him to thrash her son 'until his last miserable breath hangs only on his lips!'

'He does not even know the letter Alpha, unless someone shouts it at him five times!' complains the mother. The schoolmaster, Lampriskos, is only too ready to oblige: 'Where is my cutting switch, that bull's pizzle I use for thrashing worthless rascals? Put it in my hand, before my bile strangles me!' The thrashing proceeds, evidently enthusiastically, but eventually Lampriskos eases up because the boy is now 'striped like a water snake'. But mother calls out, 'Don't stop...Beat him until the sun goes down!' Ancient Greece was not the best place to be a recalcitrant student, it seems. It was, moreover, assumed that more punishment led to better learning, since Lampriskos suggests as an afterthought, 'Just wait; we will have him bent over a book, and give him more of it, until he learns to read better than Clio herself.'

One can see that the competing narratives that have surrounded learning haven't changed much over the millennia. In light of the *Mimes*, Plato's injunctions to put the emphasis on play rather than coercion can perhaps be seen as one of the first attempts at education reform: we can see the seeds of a debate about who children are and what we should expect from them.

The Romans maintained many of the Hellenistic traditions in schooling, a predilection for thrashing included. Augustine of Hippo in the 4th century AD notes: 'I was put to school to get learning of which I knew not what use there was; and yet, if slow to learn I was flogged.' Flogging, as we can see, really is an insistent theme: A.F. Leach divines from stray passages in Horace and Juvenal that schools were almost defined by its presence: 'The edification or cult of character...was effected by beginning school at dawn and shouting at and flogging the boys with the rod or cane (*ferula*), the tawse (*scutica*), and the birch (*flagellum*), very much as in the English schools down to 1850.' Thrashing seems to have developed almost as an art form to accompany schooling.

As you look at schools down the ages, you are forced to the conclusion that the consistency of physical punishment is surely connected with what was being expected of the young people who attended them. If children wanted to do what teachers were asking of them, would they need to be beaten? The need for beating, though, has always been a matter for deliberation, and even in ancient Rome there were disputes about its value: Quintilian, the great Roman educator, for example, disapproved of corporal punishment. (He disappointingly proceeded to suggest, though, that it was fit only for slaves—this last detracting, rather, from any inference that he might have been a liberal ahead of his time.)

Roman schooling broadly followed the Greek model. There were small schools for boys—boys only, and privileged boys to boot (and remember also that a third of the population of Rome comprised slaves), and with tutors for both boys and girls. The younger boys attended grammar schools, meaning they were taught grammar (as distinct from today's meaning of a 'grammar school', where it means 'selective school'). Then they attended rhetoric schools, where they were taught, unsurprisingly, rhetoric. The emphasis on rhetoric was because, Leach suggests, the aim of Roman education 'was to fit a boy for public life, as advocate or statesman and generally both, and this was done by training him for public speaking'.

Progress in the great journey of education fell back a bit after the fall of Rome, until, in the 8th century, Charlemagne, king of the Franks, issued his *capitulary*—sometimes called the *Charter of Modern Thought*—in which he ordered, 'Let every monastery and every abbey have its school, in which boys may be taught the Psalms, the system of musical notation, singing, arithmetic, and grammar.'

Principal among Charlemagne's intellectual advisers was Alcuin of York, who wrote manuals on grammar, rhetoric, and dialectics. It was Alcuin who developed the curriculum into the *trivium*—of grammar, logic, and rhetoric—and, following this, the *quadrivium*, of arithmetic, astronomy, geometry, and music. Together, these subjects comprised the seven liberal arts of classical study, which became the undergraduate curriculum of the first universities in Bologna, Paris, and Oxford in the 11th and 12th centuries.

The rebirth of education at this time was mainly the province of the ecclesiastical establishment, but learning of a kind (a religious kind) spilled out to the populace at large. Soon after the capitulary, Theodulf, Bishop of Orléans, had ordered that 'the priests establish schools in every town and village, and if any of the faithful wish to entrust their children to them to learn letters, that they refuse not to accept them but with all charity teach them'.

The significant changes to emerge from the mini cultural revival came not just from Charlemagne's capitulary. They came also from a new respect for rationalism as the ideas of Aristotle began to be received into the thinking of the Church through figures such as Thomas Aquinas and William of Ockham (he of the famous razor) in the 13th and 14th centuries. As rationalism began to challenge doctrine, thought was given to the nature of knowledge, inquiry, and teaching. Blueprints for forms of teaching appeared in the cathedral and monastery schools and in the universities—*lectio*, the reading of a text by a teacher, without questions, the forerunner of the lecture, and *disputatio*, the posing of a subject for dispute and debate.

Later in the Middle Ages, but before the invention of printing, other kinds of schools began to emerge. The great American educator Neil Postman suggests that these were principally associated with apprenticeship and the learning of particular trades—for there was not considered to be much else worth studying. So, there was no primary education, because until printing had made its mark on the world and reading matter was freely available there was hardly thought to be much need for any form of basic schooling in which reading and writing would be taught.

Learning was predominantly undertaken by doing, and helped along by spoken rather than written words. As Postman puts it: 'If a medieval child got to school, he would have begun as late as age ten, probably later. He would have lived on his own in lodgings in the town, far from his family. It would have been common for him to find in his class adults of all ages, and he would not have perceived himself as different from them.'

Unwillingly to school

Skip forward only a brief time to Shakespeare's Europe. It's 1575, the Renaissance sun is shining and learning has come back into fashion. By now, schools had more or less crystallized into their current form. Shakespeare's own experience at school was, if not identical to that of today's school students, broadly similar. Although Shakespeare's education would have mostly been in Latin, in 11-hour schooldays, in large classrooms divided by age, the embryo of today's schools had nevertheless become recognizable.

Why such a change in so short a time? The invention of the printing press in the 15th century had made literacy significant for far more people. Actually, I'm putting that far too weakly. I should say that the invention of printing was, for the development of thought and education, world changing, leading ultimately to the flowering of interest in art, philosophy, literature, and science that was the Renaissance. Perhaps there was too much of a good thing, though. Maybe the light was dazzling: maybe the vistas open for learning spread so wide that they made the incipient educators of the time dizzy. Like starving people faced with a banquet they wanted it all. They wanted the young to learn everything and recourse was to teaching subject upon subject, fact upon fact, and rule upon rule.

So, schools developed a curriculum, wherein important subjects—or at least subjects presumed to be important from this new panoply of riches—were taught. And the curriculum bifurcated, fanned out, and set into shape. In some ways, this broadening was, of course, a good thing. But as expectations about the curriculum hardened, the patterns that were to direct it for centuries to come were gouged into the ground.

Learning became firmly subject centred rather than child centred. And learning of the classics took pride of place in a hybrid of reverence and nostalgia for Greece and Rome. Since Latin was the language of learning, most schooling took place in it or was devoted to it. This seemed the obvious thing to do. So, after Shakespeare attended his petty school (this was more or less equivalent to our elementary and primary schools), where he learned the three Rs, he went to grammar school (high school), where the emphasis was on the study of Latin and the works of the greats: Ovid, Cicero, Virgil.

I've focused for dramatic effect on Shakespeare here, and I can assert without much fear of contradiction that literature benefited from the new learning that was happening in schools. But turning away from Shakespeare for a moment, what about his never-to-be-playwrights school chums? What use was the learning by them of Latin syntax? Already in Shakespeare's work we find a questioning of the school curriculum in the bard's mockery of some of the forms that school learning had taken. In *The Merry Wives of Windsor* (Act IV, Scene 1) he ridicules it, as the pompous schoolteacher Sir Hugh Evans interrogates young William Page:

Sir Hugh Evans:	What is 'lapis', William?
William:	A stone.
Sir Hugh Evans:	And what is 'a stone', William?
William:	A pebble.
Sir Hugh Evans:	No, it is 'lapis': I pray you, remember in your prain [brain].
William:	Lapis.
Sir Hugh Evans:	That is a good William. What is he, William, that does lend articles?

WILLIAM:	Articles are borrowed of the pronoun, and be thus declined, Singulariter, nominativo, hic, haec, hoc.
SIR HUGH EVANS:	Nominativo, hig, hag, hog; pray you, mark: genitivo, hujus. Well, what is your accusative case?
WILLIAM:	Accusativo, hinc.
SIR HUGH EVANS:	I pray you, have your remembrance, child, accusative, hung, hang, hog.

To this day the obvious often eludes us when we're deciding what should be taught at school. In Shakespeare's time, as now, much learning would inevitably for most children turn into simple drudgery, more likely killing any incipient curiosity than nurturing interest into flower. The framework for educational practice was determined for centuries to come—until today, in fact—by some not very well thought-through assumptions about what ought to be at the heart of educational practice.

What was the result of the dogged insistence on Latin conjugations? It was captured later by Shakespeare himself in *As You Like It*:

> Then the whining schoolboy, with his satchel
> And shining morning face, creeping like snail
> Unwillingly to school.

Interesting here is not just the 'whining' and the 'unwillingly' but their juxtaposition with the 'shining morning face'. Shakespeare manages to contrast the bright eagerness of youth with what school did, and so often still does—pinching out the flames of curiosity, creativity, and inventiveness.

Calls for change

Once upon a time, things had been so simple: young people learned all the stuff they needed to learn for a trade or calling; there was a clear purpose involved. Then the Renaissance had come along and offered a cornucopia of learning for the delectation of the already learned. Learning to think for oneself, so valued by Plato, became buried beneath this welter of opportunities—opportunities which became sterile imperatives.

But voices were emerging saying that things could be different, renewing questions that the Ancients had raised about the purpose of education. The learning for learning's sake of Shakespeare's schooling began to be questioned. Some teachers, such as Elizabeth I's tutor, Roger Ascham (1515–68), promoted learning-by-doing in *The Scholemaster*: 'Bring not up your children in learning by compulsion and feare,' he said, 'but by playing and pleasure.' Likewise, William Petty, a doctor in Cromwell's army in 1647, noted that '...we see children do delight in drums, pipes, fiddles, guns made of elder sticks, and bellowes noses, piped keys, etc., painting flags and ensigns with elder-berries and corn poppy, making ships with paper, and setting even nut-shells a swimming, handling the tools of workmen as soon as they turn their backs, and trying to work themselves' (reported in the Harleian Miscellany, 1810).

One of the first to think systematically about all of this, urging a pause for thought about why we were actually teaching children, was the Czech teacher Comenius (1592–1670). He championed universal education, which he promoted in his *Didactica magna*, arguing for the commonality of education—it was for everyone, including, shockingly, females. (Comenius's concern for the need for universal education, including that of girls and women, makes one realize just how *un*concerned everyone else had been about the education of half of the population.) Strikingly in tune with our thought today, he argued for education's continuing nature: it didn't begin and end at specified ages. And in his insistence on pitching the right work at the right level he was a forerunner of much that later thinkers went on to say: 'Nothing should be taught to the young...unless it is not only permitted, but actually demanded by their age and mental strength.'

It's telling that the questions being raised by folk such as Comenius didn't really hit the public consciousness until a couple of hundred years later: until, that is, they were made understandable by someone who could communicate. Enter the Swiss political philosopher and polymath Jean-Jacques Rousseau, who shocked the world with *Émile: or On Education* ([1762] 1993). Émile is the eponymous pupil-hero of Rousseau's treatise on childrearing and education; his book contains passages such as this:

> Instead of keeping [Émile] mewed up in a stuffy room, take him out into a meadow every day; let him run about, let him struggle and fall again and again, the oftener the better; he will learn all the sooner to pick himself up... My pupil will hurt himself oftener than yours, but he will always be merry; your pupils may receive fewer injuries, but they are always thwarted, constrained, and sad.
>
> Rousseau 1993: 49

These were revolutionary and exciting ideas about education, and *Émile* flew off the shelves in 18th-century Paris. In fact booksellers found it more profitable to rent it out by the hour than to sell it. Ultimately the excitement got too much for the authorities and *Émile* was banned in Paris and burned in Geneva. Rousseau's heretical view was that anything which was outside children's experience would be meaningless to them, much as Plato, Comenius, and others had warned. His insights had condensed principally out of the prevailing intellectual atmosphere at the time—empiricism, explicated by philosophers such as John Locke. We'll look at Locke and Rousseau in more detail in Chapter 2.

Although Rousseau had an influence on a handful of European educators, it would be misleading to imply that the impact on education of these new ideas about learning through discovery was, at the time, profound. Fascinating though his ideas seemed to be to many people, they barely made a puncture mark on the developing institution of school. Things continued in much the same way as they had before, with recitations of lists of facts and the chanting of Latin conjugations all the way up to the advent of universal compulsory schooling toward the end of the 19th century, and things didn't change all that much after this either.

After Victoria

There is a Marxist analysis of what happens now in the development of schooling, and this is well explained by Samuel Bowles and Herbert Gintis in their classic *Schooling in Capitalist America*. (Actually, although Bowles and Gintis say 'in...America' in the title, you could change this for 'everywhere in the newly industrialized world'.) Schools now became instruments of the dominant economic system: capitalism. The industrial–military machine became the executive director and the school its servant. Capitalism needed workers who possessed and could use particular kinds of knowledge; schools provided them.

The theme of the Marxists' analysis is familiar, but the analysis should not be dismissed: there is plenty of evidence for its validity. One can take as a little case study in its support the discussion at the time about Forster's Act in 1870, which mandated education for all children up to the age of 10 in Britain. Before this legislation, school attendance had not been compulsory and only about half of the population attended schools; indeed, the proportion was even lower in rural areas, where children's labour was vital for family income. But we know from comments made in Parliament at the time that the new law in 1870 was passed not out of a feeling that the populace needed to have its mind opened; the stimulus came neither from the love of learning nor from a desire to awaken in the consciousness of the workers the glories of antiquity or the marvels revealed by science.

Nothing so noble. Rather, the stimulus came from a worry about the nation losing its competitive edge because of the lack of a workforce with basic education. Both the USA and Prussia had already provided free, compulsory elementary education, and the Americans were, as the 20th century began, even providing universal secondary schooling. European schools were ousting classical subjects and replacing them with engineering and science. For many, the mere thought was outrageous, but it was clear that the European and US competitors were benefiting from these changes to the curriculum in advances in commerce, in industry, and even on the battlefield. As the UK prime minister William Gladstone put it at the time in the *Edinburgh Review*, speaking of the remarkable Prussian success in the Franco–Prussian War: 'Undoubtedly, the conduct of the campaign, on the German side, has given a marked triumph to the cause of systematic popular education.'

So the rationale behind compulsory schooling was instrumental: it came from the expectation that it would lead to industrial and even military success. And as mass production took over in the factory, it is far from fanciful to suggest that schools themselves began to look more like factories, with standardization of practices, specialization in the curriculum, and professionalization of the workforce.

One of the criticisms raised about the analysis proffered by Bowles and Gintis is that what happens in schools is far from being a tame process of industry feeding. Indeed, many teachers would argue that they do their best to engender a critical, thinking disposition in their students. But the political case for school has to this day resolutely centred around 'standards' and 'outcomes', with an ever-burgeoning array of tests to assess students' performance in what the CBI ('The voice of business' in the UK) calls 'employability skills'. Rarely do we hear politicians talking about schools failing in their duty to help children become critical thinkers. As the social historian G.M. Trevelyan (1978) put the issue some time ago, 'Education...has produced a vast population able to read but unable to distinguish what is worth reading.'

It's a basic question—What are children and young people in school *for*?—that stands behind Trevelyan's comment, and it has dominated discussion about education not just for the last 50 or 100 years, but, as we have seen, for ever. We have continually to think about the aims and ideals of education and not just the processes by which it is provided. Those aims and ideals are at the core of the debate about progressive education, which I examine next.

Chapter 2
Oil and water: the formal and the progressive

From Plato's Academy to the schools of today, some key questions have remained unresolved. Should schools principally be about passing on knowledge and skills to a new generation, and if so which knowledge and which skills? Or should they put the emphasis on the transmission of the manners, habits, and traditions of a culture? Should education be about encouraging compliance with the existing ideas and norms of a society or should it concern the promotion of a questioning, challenging, free-thinking disposition?

Put starkly, the big debate in education is about how much the emphasis should be on the learning of facts and how much it should be on the encouragement of thinking. This is how Charles Dickens, as great an educational reformer as he was a novelist, saw the emphasis on facts in this portrait of the frightening teacher Mr Gradgrind in *Hard Times*:

> 'Now, what I want is, Facts. Teach these boys and girls nothing but Facts. Facts alone are wanted in life. Plant nothing else, and root out everything else. You can only form the minds of reasoning animals upon Facts: nothing else will ever be of any service to them. This is the principle on which I bring up my own children, and this is the principle on which I bring up these children. Stick to Facts, sir!…Give me your definition of a horse.'

(Sissy Jupe thrown into the greatest alarm by this demand.)

'Girl number twenty unable to define a horse!' said Mr. Gradgrind... 'Girl number twenty possessed of no facts, in reference to one of the commonest of animals! Some boy's definition of a horse. Bitzer, yours.'...

'Quadruped. Graminivorous. Forty teeth, namely twenty-four grinders, four eye-teeth, and twelve incisive. Sheds coat in the spring; in marshy countries, sheds hoofs, too. Hoofs hard, but requiring to be shod with iron. Age known by marks in mouth.' ...

'Now girl number twenty,' said Mr. Gradgrind. 'You know what a horse is.'

Of course, the point Dickens was making was that Bitzer did not 'know' what a horse was from this definition and nor was poor Sissy Jupe likely to gain much from Bitzer's learned-by-heart explication. Bitzer and Sissy Jupe were already amply aware of what horses were from their routine experience of life—every day seeing them and hearing the clatter of their feet on the cobbles. Gradgrind's 'facts' helped not a jot in their understanding.

Teaching facts versus the encouragement of thinking: the tension between these has been a peculiarly hard-wearing one through the long journey of organized education.

Two sets of ideas: two traditions

There's nothing new about controversies about what education should be about. Take what Aristotle had to say in the 4th century BC:

For in modern times there are opposing views about the tasks to be set, for there are no generally accepted assumptions about what the young should learn, either for virtue or for the best life; nor yet is it clear whether their education ought to be conducted with more concern for the intellect than for the character of the soul. The problem has been complicated by the education we see actually given; and it is by no means certain whether training should be directed at things useful in life, or at those conducive to virtue, or at exceptional accomplishments. (All these answers have been judged correct by somebody.)

Aristotle, *The Politics*, VIII, ii, 1337a33

So, it was not yet 'clear' what the focus of education should be—the development of the intellect, virtue, or 'accomplishment'. And two millennia later it's still not clear: Aristotle's commentary seems fresh and relevant today.

Among the contradictory positions to which Aristotle alludes are intermingled two streams of thought which run through the history of education—they are usually called the *progressive* and the *formal*. (Actually, they go under many names but we'll stick with these for now.) They have lain alongside each other for centuries, but there has been little intercourse. Never mind intercourse, any kind of relationship would be tough, since these traditions grew out of entirely different world views, entirely different assumptions about knowledge and about learning.

The differences between these schools of thought can perhaps be summed up in a further set of questions, the answers to which reveal that there are not only different understandings about knowledge and learning held by the protagonists of each position, but also different views about children—who they are and how they develop. Those questions can be summarized as follows:

- How should we view knowledge? Is there a stock of knowledge which we need to record, accumulate, and pass on to the next generation? Or is knowledge fluid and transitory, most useful when it is personally discovered and acquired?

- How should we view learning? Is it demonstrated by the proven acquisition of facts and skills, or by the demonstration of a facility with reasoning and solving problems?

- And how should we view children? (Rightly or wrongly, it is children about whom we are principally concerned when we think about education.) Do we see them principally as members of a society and participants in an economy for which they need to be prepared—as adults in the making? Or is our role in their development to think less about *preparation* and more about *cultivation*? Should we, in other words, see children as independent and differently reasoning individuals who, through their ingenuity and their differences, will come to contribute in many and varied ways to the cultures of which they are a part?

Let me look at the two world views in the light of these questions.

The progressives

I introduced Jean-Jacques Rousseau in Chapter 1. I think it is fair to say that the questions I've just outlined didn't really crystallize in the public consciousness until this Swiss polymath published *Émile* in the middle of the 18th century. His ideas laid the foundation for much that has followed in the way of progressive thinking and they sprang from his view of the child as different from the adult—as open-minded: an eager, ready learner. Children learn from experience, he observed, not from being force-fed facts. They are little scientists, learning empirically— learning from their trial-and-error dealings with the world. More than this, their open, receptive minds are particularly suited to learning from experience, in the way that adults' minds often are not. Where adult thinking has set hard into shape and is disinclined to change, children's thinking is characterized by plasticity. It moulds itself to the experiences it encounters.

This view of the child as a mini experimenter was in tune with the new empirical take on philosophy that was happening in Rousseau's day. Empiricism was the new intellectual trend. Before this, just about any difficult question on any subject at all could find a perfectly acceptable answer in authority of one kind or another—in 'It is God's will,' rather than 'Let's find out.' Things were beginning to change, though, as empiricist philosophers were daring to suggest that real knowledge could be gained only from experience—from the evidence of our eyes and ears, from our trial-and-error dealings with the world and from experiments of one kind or another. It was a new view: a scientific view; an Enlightenment view.

A particularly influential character in the developing philosophy of empiricism and the Enlightenment was the English philosopher John Locke, who had interested himself in education and had published in 1693 *Some Thoughts Concerning Education* a few decades before Rousseau's *Émile*. Locke's short treatise on education was based on a series of letters to his friend Edward Clarke on the education of Mr and Mrs Clarke's children. Not only does Locke provide an intellectual foundation for Rousseau's view of the child as an experimenter, we can also see the seeds of Rousseau's notions of the plasticity of the child's mind in comments such as 'I imagine the minds of children as easily turned this or that way as water itself.'

Before talking about the richness of Locke's insights on the child-as-empiricist, I should note that there was, alongside the insightful, some distinctly odd advice in *Some Thoughts Concerning Education*. For a start, there is this: '*Melons, peaches* and most sorts of *plums*, and all sorts of *grapes* in England, I think children should be *wholly kept from* as having a very tempting taste in a very unwholesome juice' (p 20, original emphases). Strangely, though, given the warnings about 'tempting taste' and 'unwholesome juice', Locke thought it was just fine for children to eat strawberries, cherries, gooseberries, or currants (as long as they were ripe, he added, for the avoidance of doubt). He even offered grim warnings about children's bowel movements, stressing the absolute need for regularity. Regularity should not be achieved, however, at the expense of density or compactness in the, ahem, product, for 'People that are very *loose* have seldom strong thoughts or strong bodies' (p 22, original emphasis).

It might perhaps be thought strange that one of the founding fathers of empiricism seems to have considered it perfectly acceptable to offer guidance on matters such as this without any empirical evidence whatever for his advice, but we'll let that pass. Locke's great insight is in his recognition of the child as special—as an eager ingénue, ready to learn by discovering knowledge. It is children's 'tractableness' (p 63), as he puts it, that is especially of interest and this meshes with his view of knowledge as learned from experience, rather than acquired by way of authority. It was a new way of looking at the way we all learn, and in particular the way that the child learns. Because children are tractable—because their minds are blank slates (or *tabulae rasae* as Locke famously put it)—they are primed and ready, if you like, for empiricism. They are ready for learning by discovery, by seeking evidence.

It is this new view of the child as a different *kind* of learner which we take from Locke. It's a hugely important one. Amidst the somewhat peculiar counsel on ripe fruit, there is in Locke the seed of a very different and important new take on learning—one which is based on observations and understandings about the way that children actually learn...or fail to learn. Take, for example, what he says about learning to read: 'great care is to be taken that it be never made as a business to him, nor he look on it as a task. We naturally...even from our cradles, love liberty and have therefore an aversion to many things for no other reason but because they are enjoined us' (p 113). We get switched off, Locke is saying, by being told to do things. When it came to learning, Locke, like Plato 2,000 years before, was against compulsion and in favour of fun. 'Make it a game' was surely his motto.

Remember that Locke wrote *Some Thoughts Concerning Education* in 1693, just after Samuel Butler had made the phrase 'Spare the rod and spoil the child' immortal in his satirical poem *Hudibras*. There wasn't anything much more profound than 'Spare the rod' at the time: it was the essence of good child-rearing advice and not much had changed since schoolmaster Lampriskos's reliance on his trusty bull's pizzle 2,000 years earlier. By contrast, in what looks like counsel for the beginning of modern nursery practice, Locke offers games such as the making of dice that have letters of the alphabet on them for the amusement and encouragement of children. He even suggests, in advice that would make our modern secretaries of state for education shudder, that parents and teachers shouldn't become concerned to push their charges too early into the learning of reading. Leave it a bit, he suggests: ''Tis better it be a year later *before he can read*, than that he should this way get an aversion to learning' (p 116).

How true, and how prescient, given that the country which now has the best literacy achievement in the world among its young people is Finland—and it turns out that Finland has one of the latest school start ages in the world. Children don't begin school until they are seven years old, yet they have the best reading. Yes, Locke's 'leave it a bit' is good advice. (Incidentally, this Finnish phenomenon—best reading, latest school start age—is sometimes called the 'Finnish paradox'. In fact, it's only a paradox if you believe that the best way to help learning along is methodically to hammer information into children at every possible opportunity and from the earliest possible age—preferably in the womb.)

Locke's views on education grew not just out of his observations about the way children thought, but also out of his views on politics and society. We could say that he was the first progressive educator not simply because he encouraged his contemporaries and successors to think about the child as a special kind of learner, but also because of his views on education's role in helping to develop an open, liberal polity. A political system, he said, needs people who are fair, open-minded and think for themselves; it doesn't want people who are subservient to authority.

In his essay *Of the Conduct of the Understanding*, Locke frowned upon those 'who seldom reason at all, but do and think according to the example of others, whether parents, neighbours, ministers...for the saving of themselves the pains and trouble of thinking and examining for themselves' (p 169). In all of this he concurred with Aristotle, who had said, many centuries before in *Politics* (Book VIII): 'No one would dispute the fact that it is a lawgiver's prime duty to arrange for the education of the young. In states where this is not done the quality of the constitution suffers.'

For Locke, openness and intellectual interchange would help to counter the overweening influence on politics of the church and the aristocracy. His ideas were to have a profound influence on political life in general and on the shaping of the American constitution in particular. In a way, Locke is emblematic of the deeper connection between education and politics: education has always been of interest to those who want to change and improve society—or, indeed, those who wish to preserve it from disruption or forgetfulness (as we shall see in a moment when we come to the formalists).

Locke and Rousseau separately built the foundations for the modern move to a different kind of education. I say 'the modern move' since there had existed, as we have seen, similar thinking long before. But those earlier ideas had been lost somewhere along the way until they were rediscovered by these pioneers of the modern movement. In fact, they did more than merely breathe life into the ancient wisdoms about education: they gave a detailed rationale for the likely benefits of their adoption.

Although the new ideas received a mixed reception over the following 300 years, the spark had kindled new thought and activity about education, and a few enthusiasts for the cause shifted the ground forward in a variety of new, experimental schools. Among those enthusiasts, first, there was another Swiss: Johann Pestalozzi. Admiring Rousseau (indeed, even naming his only son Jean-Jacques after the maestro), Pestalozzi pushed the master's ideas along, incorporating them with those of others— Aristotle, Bacon, Comenius—drawing out the practical consequences of their ideas. He opened his own schools, using the methods advocated by Rousseau and others and developing his own. He expounded these in the not-too-catchily titled *How Gertrude Teaches her Children*. Pestalozzi kept to Rousseau's ideas about the significance of exploration and observation but wrapped this in a holistic view of the child—one which integrated heart and head—and which placed tenderness and respect for children at the centre of education. Allowing no corporal punishment in any of his schools, he suggested that without care and warmth, 'neither the physical nor the intellectual powers will develop naturally'.

A little later, Friedrich Froebel, a German student of Pestalozzi, who spent time observing at Pestalozzi's school, edged things forward again, with an emphasis on the education of younger children. If you have ever wondered where the odd word 'kindergarten' comes from, look no further than Froebel. Coined by him on a walk one day in the Thuringian hills, and meaning 'children's garden' or 'garden of children', the word 'kindergarten' is now used the world over to describe preschool or nursery education. He published *Die Menschenerziehung* (*The Education of Man*) in 1826, which stresses practical, creative activity and play and the way in which education continues from preschool to adulthood and beyond. It was to be a process of cultivation, not transmission, with education resting in the support and nurture of the child's ready-made talents. Out of the ideas of Pestalozzi and Froebel, in the early 1900s Maria Montessori developed her method, depending on practical tasks such as personal care and care for the environment, putting independence at the centre of the curriculum. Her method was quite widely adopted for a time in both Europe and America.

The ideas of the progressives were taken forward only patchily, though: there was never a mass movement for progressive education. While the dashing Rousseau had mightily excited the bewigged ladies of 18th-century Paris (who kept miniatures of him in their lockets) there was a resistance to introducing his and his followers' ideas to mainstream practice. All this stuff about freedom was a bit too radical. And things didn't change much over the following century. Moves toward wholesale progressive schooling were usually taken to be experimental and a bit hippyish, and they happened disconnectedly, in small private enterprises. One of these was the Hampstead School, which opened in 1897 to put into practice the 'best theories of education extant', particularly those of 'Pestalozzi, Froebel . . . Louis Compton Miall, and others working on similar lines'. There was to be cooperation between parents and teachers and the curriculum stressed interest rather than memory. There would be no competition or punishment and, perhaps nodding at the fringe nature of progressive education, vegetarian dinners were to be provided (see Cockburn et al.).

John Dewey's Laboratory School was founded in 1896 with the aim of providing the kind of progressive education that it was not possible to find in other schools in the USA at the time. He started with sixteen pupils from the Hyde Park area of Chicago near the university. Dewey's aim was to create a school which would be a cooperative community in which the mechanical and repetitive drill methods of teaching would be replaced by learning through projects to do with real-life activity. We'll come to Professor Dewey again in Chapter 4.

Formal versus progressive

While there is a range of thinkers who have encouraged us in the progressive direction, there is no equivalent cadre of big-hitting thinkers linked with the formal position. It's as if the formal has always been there, for it is the common-sense foil against which the progressive position emerged to question and contest. If there is a core theme to the formal position it is that education is about passing on information; for formalists, culture and civilization represent a store of ideas and wisdom which have to be handed on to new generations. Teaching is at the heart of this transmission; and the process of transmission *is* education.

While progressive educators stress the child's development from within, formalists put the emphasis, by contrast, on formation from without—formation that comes from immersion in the knowledge, ideas, beliefs, concepts, and visions of society, culture, civilization. There are, one might say, conservative and liberal interpretations of this world view—the conservative putting the emphasis on *transmission* itself, on telling, and the liberal putting the emphasis more on *induction*, on initiation by involvement with culture's established ideas. This latter notion of education is discussed with most sophistication and elegance by the 20th-century philosopher Michael Oakeshott (though it would be simplistic to call Oakeshott a formalist—the labels break down, rather, as the discussion about these issues becomes more nuanced). Oakeshott saw education as part of the 'conversation of mankind', wherein teachers induct their students into that conversation by teaching them how to participate in the dialogue—how to hear the 'voices' of previous generations while cultivating their own unique voices.

What are some of the broader principles formalists defend, when looked at next to those of a progressive persuasion?

Education: leading out ... or acquiring skills and knowledge?

For the progressives, education is about supporting the ability to think critically: it should be child centred and focused on problem solving. For the formalists, though, it's a process of imparting and acquiring the skills and knowledge necessary for wellbeing and success in life. It's about instruction and the acquisition of information and skills needed for the success of the society in which you live.

Learning: easy ... or hard?

For progressives, learning is natural; it's happening all the time and it's what humans are programmed for. Children learn to talk, for example, without any teaching at all. Progressive educators say that this learning of language provides us with a lesson: it shows that we are almost hard-wired for complex learning—it comes easily, if the circumstances for its acquisition are right. We should make use of this strength, putting children in positions where they have the opportunity to think rather than telling them *what* to think.

For formalists, though, learning is, sadly, hard slog. No pain, no gain. They contend that it is just a fact of life that there are some things that you need to learn the hard way. There is complex information that we need to know to which there is no easy route. If you want to learn to write, for example, you need to understand the ways in which language is put together; you need to know the glue that binds sentences—the rules for making language work. This isn't easy, and you don't 'discover' it.

Discovery ... or authority?

While the progressives think of education involving discovery and play, the formalists say that to put the emphasis on discovery is to ignore the tapestry of established ideas, rules, and traditions that have been handed down to us from countless earlier generations. It's such a rich picture, developed painfully with false starts and dead ends over the millennia, that we are wrong to expect children independently to discover its facts for themselves. The rules of language, the laws of nature, the theorems of geometry are not for discovery—they need to be imparted, delivered. There are many things that we have to take on trust; every minute of every day we have to accept the testimony and the guidance of those who are in a position to offer an authoritative view.

There's no shame or intellectual dishonesty in doing this, say the formalists. It's all very well to say that we learn things best when we discover them for ourselves, but this is to deny the heritage of ideas that go to constitute just about every understanding of contemporary life. If you 'discover' how light is broken into the colours of the rainbow by a prism, for example, you aren't really discovering it—you are, in unearthing this little revelation, incorporating an iceberg's worth of associated work and understandings which in reality you are taking on trust: you are accepting it on the word of authority.

And, proceed the formalists, given that there are better ways and worse ways of doing things, should education really be about expecting children to battle through the worse ways before learning the better ways? Why not shortcut the process so that confusing diversions are avoided and sloppy thinking habits not induced? Isn't it in fact something close to sadism not to teach learners the elements of a task rather than expect them to find out through trial and error?

While discovery helps learners to gain some ownership of what is being learned—because they feel that they have found out something for themselves, and therefore 'own' the knowledge— this is only part of the process of learning, the formalists say. Where children don't have the scaffolding of associated ideas and mental models to help them hold the new knowledge in place, anything that they discover is as good as useless. They don't realize where one bit connects to another, or why it matters if they are seen to connect. They need a structure that acts to frame new knowledge—that holds it in place for them and indicates where and why one bit leads to the next.

Questioning vs structure and security

The progressive approach seeks to develop a questioning mind in young people. Aside from the fact that it is at the heart of a scientific disposition to be questioning and doubtful, we need to encourage a critical and challenging mindset for good social and political reasons as well. We need always to hold our politicians, leaders, and others in authority to account and education is a central means of developing the critical disposition that enables us to do this.

Formalists would agree on the need of a questioning populace— one that doesn't take priests' and politicians' word for it (whatever 'it' is). But they say that the tender years of childhood are not the

Education

time to try and encourage this outlook. If we see children as different from adults, we should accept that they don't need or want to be questioning; they don't need or want doubt. Rather, they need security, structure, and authority. In fact, they actively like to know where they stand, and not to have to make decisions about difficult issues.

Apprenticeship ... or teaching? Individuals, groups or the whole class?

Where advocates of a progressive approach suggest that children learn best one-to-one with a teacher, or in a group, formalists argue that this is, in either case, impracticable, given that there is one teacher to twenty or thirty children. What is to be done with all of the others when you are teaching one-to-one?

Motivation from within ... or without?

How are young learners motivated to do a task? How does curiosity become aroused and the attention focused? The progressives say that the only kind of meaningful motivation comes through interest and absorption in the task or subject itself: it's called 'intrinsic motivation' in the jargon. Children should want to do an activity because it interests them.

Formalists say that this is a counsel of perfection and doesn't marry with the real world: some subjects are as dull as ditchwater, and there's no getting round it. One could, perhaps with a heroic effort on the part of the teacher, manage to make chemistry's periodic table interesting, but the reality is that the facts needed to understand the periodic table are hard work. The motivation to learn it has to be external—or, again in the jargon, 'extrinsic motivation'—by encouragement to learn through classroom rewards, the praise and approval of the teacher, the desire to achieve better grades, reporting to parents, and other kinds of incentives, rewards, and sanctions. More than this, say the formalists, doing difficult and boring things is part of the real world, and children have to get used to it.

Table 1: Progressive versus formal education

	Progressive education	Formal education
Also known as …	Informal; child centred; discovery learning; open education; integrated day; new education; learning by doing	Traditional; teacher directed; didactic; 'back to basics'; essentialism; 'chalk and talk'
Achieves aims by …	Problem solving; activity; discovery; play	Instruction; learning facts, established ideas, rules and traditions; compliance
Aims to …	Teach the child to think, to be independent, to be critical	Teach the child the skills and knowledge necessary for life
Assumes that children, above all, need …	Freedom	Structure
Curriculum is …	Project based or topic based, with the integration of 'subjects'	Subject based, with subjects taught separately
Emphasizes …	Activity, freedom, and the growth of understanding; individuality; the nature of the child	Teaching; reception and acquisition of knowledge and skill; conformity to established principles of conduct and inquiry; the nature of knowledge

Motivation by …	Absorption in the work itself; the satisfaction gained by working with others—cooperation	A desire to comply with teacher demands; competition for better grades; rewards and punishments
Motto (after Dewey, in *Experience and Education*) …	Development from within	Formation from without
Students and pupils relating with the teacher mainly by …	Group or individual work, with teachers and pupils in a mentor–apprentice relationship	Mainly whole-class work, with the teacher primarily in an instructional position
What to be learned …	How to think independently; critical thinking; a questioning disposition	Basic skills; factual information and principles; respect for authority

I've been calling these two approaches the 'progressive' and the 'formal' approaches, but they have gone under a variety of names: progressive, informal, child centred on the one side; formal, traditional, teacher directed on the other. Table 1 sums up the differences.

In one of his later works, *Experience and Education*, Dewey regretted the slipping into camps that had come out of the vituperative discussion of progressive versus formal education. He said that we 'should think in terms of Education itself rather than in terms of some 'ism about education, even such an 'ism as "progressivism"' (p 6). Allegiance to an 'ism, he suggested, became almost tribal, so that one's time was spent arguing against the rival 'ism rather than constructively striving to face actual problems and real needs. Concentrate, said Dewey, not on the 'ism but on the experiences that children actually have in the settings we provide for their education. We should strive to pass on the traditions of human thinking while teaching new generations how to engage critically with those traditions and revise them.

Chapter 3
The traditions unfold: ideas into practice

In practice, few schools and fewer teachers fall neatly into the categories, progressive or formal, that I have outlined. In reality there is an acceptance that each position has some validity, that each has an intellectual hinterland. So it's not really so much a question of either/or but, rather, 'How much of each?' There is a continuum wherein different schools take differing amounts from each tradition. A no-holds-barred progressivism is at one end—one could perhaps put here a school such as Summerhill, where the students are obliged only to follow student-made rules. Strict formalism is at the other; perhaps some of the Islamic madrassas, which focus exclusively on the learning of scriptures, could be put here. In between are the great majority of schools, which draw from both sets of understandings.

Teachers in primary schools have tended to take from the progressive tradition more than their secondary colleagues. If you look at the arrangement of furniture in almost any primary classroom you will find it organized for the assumption of cooperation, discussion, and activity more than is the case in the secondary school. In Burke and Grosvenor's *The School I'd Like*, pupil Joanna (thirteen years old) put it this way about the arrangements that still operate in many secondary schools:

Even in the 21st century in schools pupils sit in rows like the Victorians. You can only talk to the person next to you (this is probably why the teachers make us sit in rows); this means that in discussion work which is extremely important in today's society ideas and suggestions don't come as quickly.

Classrooms and groupwork

But it's different for younger children: visitors to the modern state primary school classroom almost anywhere in the Western world will see the children arranged in groups, and the arrangement is the fruit of progressive thinkers' influence. The idea is that children should, in their groups, be able to do groupwork, and in doing this groupwork they should be able to talk, cooperate, share ideas, experiment. This is the way that we learn, say the progressive educators—actively and socially, with others and through others.

One of the most celebrated examples of this approach to primary education is to be found in the area around the northern Italian region of Reggio Emilia. Here, after the destruction and internal rifts brought by the Second World War in that country, parents, teachers, and community resolved to build a new kind of education based on cooperation, community spirit, and solidarity. The approach ultimately adopted is a fine example of the ways in which education is often shaped by some quite profound assumptions about what people are like, and how civilization can be preserved.

The Reggio Emilia approach has become world famous. Originating at more or less the same time as changes to ideas about curriculum and styles of teaching in the UK and the USA, it especially caught the imagination of educators worldwide for its energy and for the commitment invested by all in the community to make it a success. It combined the discovery approaches of the progressive educators with a dedication to community

2. The Reggio Emilia approach is sometimes taken to be the exemplar of the progressive, project-based method

involvement and especially the involvement of parents in education. It blended this with a stress on the importance of the layout of the physical space of the school, always organizing this in such a way that it would encourage encounters and communication between children and adults in groups.

Such groupwork has been at the cornerstone of much primary practice, but it is more difficult to put into practice than the success of the Reggio Emilia project might suggest. When you look at what happens in practice in many schools—when you look at what students are being asked to do when they are put into groups to work—as often as not they are *not* actually doing groupwork. Rather, they are probably being asked by the teacher to do work on their own based on a class lesson or worksheets— but to do it while sitting in a group.

This raises some serious issues. The very features of groups which make them good for cooperation and communication also make

35

them poor for doing individual work, because students can easily make eye contact with the person opposite, talk to the person next to them, and generally get distracted from that individual work. That was the point of putting them in groups: to encourage them to talk. But work that requires concentrated individual effort is best done in a setting which minimizes distraction.

When research first appeared showing the kind of *individual* work children were doing in *groups*, formalists argued that it demonstrated that primary school teachers' acceptance of a progressive philosophy is, in practice, only skin deep. Progressive practice, they said, is so difficult actually to accomplish given the constraints and exigencies of classroom life that teachers fall back on doing traditional chalk-and-talk activity, while presenting the impression—but only the impression—of the groupwork associated with discovery learning. The result, they say, is individual work done in groups—and this represents the worst of both worlds since the individual work just gets done badly.

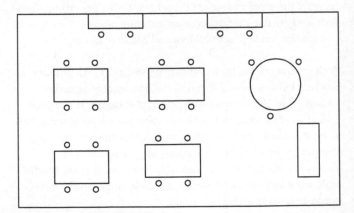

3. A typical primary classroom arranged in groups. But are the children doing group work?

The hybrid nature of much practice raises perennial questions about adjustments in practice—whether to become more or less formal, more or less progressive. And the pendulum, among teachers as in the national mood, swings one way then the other. In discussions about this—about which approach offers the route to best practice—the temptation has sometimes been to try to resolve the debate rationally, through research. Surely research should be able to tell us which educational approaches have better outcomes.

It's not quite that simple, though, since the terms of reference for the debate spin around what we mean by 'outcomes'. If empirical research told us, for example, that segregating children by ability, gender, disability, or ethnicity yielded benefits for young people's academic achievement, how should we proceed? (It doesn't tell us this, incidentally, but let's just imagine for a moment.) Would this finding encourage us to segregate our schools—to make them un-comprehensive? Or would our knowledge about the corrosive effects of segregation instead drive us to seek better ways of teaching in unsegregated classes?

Or take the notion of quality of thinking, so fought over by the proponents of each tradition. The problem here is not with priorities and values but with our understanding of 'quality': it's going to be mighty hard to come to any agreement on what we mean by it. My idea of quality in thinking, involving persistence, understanding, and imagination, may differ from yours, which may stress accuracy, speed, and memory. The researcher is faced with an array of interlocking concerns in a question such as this, and even if some of them are amenable to empirical investigation, there will remain a great deal of room for argument about any findings concerning quality of thinking. The problem is that the adoption of one approach over another involves our priorities and values, and empirical research can give us only limited assistance in filling in facts.

But even those 'facts' are difficult to come by and are open to big differences of interpretation. Take one of the distinctions I raised in Table 1 in the previous chapter—that of growth of understanding versus the reception and acquisition of knowledge and skill. You may find that one method for teaching reading, which emphasizes the breaking down of words into their component parts, initially has more success, with 'success' measured by proficiency in recognizing words, than another approach. That other approach may stress learners' enjoyment of reading, where the teacher's emphasis is on the interest, attractiveness, and meaningfulness of the reading material. The first approach may seem to bear most fruit initially but the latter approach may encourage learners to enjoy reading, use it productively and pay the greatest dividends in the long run.

Or think about another of the distinctions I raised in Table 1, discovery versus authority. If you try to find out which is better—encouraging children to discover by experimenting with prisms how white light splits into colours versus telling them authoritatively about it—you are immediately into problems about *kind* of learning. Even if a formal educator is able to show better results on a test given to children about the colours into which light is split, the progressive educator will be able to retort with 'Yes, but what do the children actually *understand* about the splitting of light?' They would be making the point that their charges, who had been informally experimenting with prisms, may not be able to parrot 'red, orange, yellow, green, blue, indigo, violet' or some other easily measureable outcome, but they would appreciate how light divides by having actively experimented. They might even be inspired to find out more.

Both of these examples raise an important point. The tests and measurements we choose to employ in trying to answer questions such as this may actually themselves influence practice. If there is undue emphasis on easily measured indicators (as there has been in recent years all over the world as governments have insisted on greater accountability from teachers), this in itself is going to have an effect on the shape and style of the education on offer to children. Teachers will 'teach to the test'—and if the test comprises the most easily measured outcomes, as it nearly always does, this will result in the teaching focusing on those outcomes.

Foregrounding some of these issues is an iconic piece of research done in 1967 by a team based at the University of Lancaster, in England. Focusing specifically on the formal–progressive question, it divided teachers according to the styles they adopted (broadly, formal and progressive) and then looked at the outcomes of the children in their classes. In brief, it concluded that children who were in open, informal classrooms where the teaching was predominantly progressive learned less in English, maths, and reading than did those in formal classrooms. It was reported in Neville Bennett's *Teaching Styles and Pupil Progress*, and Bennett concluded his work with these words:

> In summary, formal teaching fulfils its aims in the academic area without detriment to the social and emotional development of pupils. Whereas informal teaching only partially fulfils its aims in the latter area as well as engendering comparatively poorer outcomes in academic development. (p 162)

The work was reported widely and was hugely influential. It represented a serious blow for progressive educators.

But they didn't just sulk. They scrutinized the methods that Bennett had used to come to his conclusions. Were teachers in each group equivalent in experience—might those teachers in the formal group tend to be, for whatever reason, more experienced? Were the groups balanced in their social class construction? (If they weren't, with the formal teaching styles tending to be found in more socially advantaged areas, the findings could have been influenced by this.) Such questions forced a re-examination of the data and entirely different findings were made on re-analysis.

Differences between the groups turned out to be far smaller, and they didn't all point in the same direction. Some findings seemed to point to the superiority of formal teaching, for example in English, while others (in reading) suggested that informal classrooms produced better results. For maths there was no clear difference.

Whatever the re-analysis found, should people have been swayed in their attitudes to different kinds of teaching by Bennett's findings? If research indicates that in a formal classroom children seem to do better in the basic skills, isn't this what one would expect? It's surely not surprising if teachers who teach basic skills systematically, giving a good deal of time and attention to the task, teach those skills more productively than those who instead prioritize children's ability to understand, imagine, and create. If we assessed 'outcomes' by focusing on understanding and creativity, perhaps those children in classes with informal teachers would have fared better.

The various questions that arose from Bennett's research led to more complex research that sought to understand what teachers were actually doing in their organization and what the consequences of this happened to be. One of the issues that had arisen was that it had proved difficult baldly to define teachers as formal or progressive. So, researchers worked on more sophisticated understandings of the ways that teachers worked. What were the lineaments of formality or informality?

One of the most important pieces of research into this question came from project ORACLE, which involved making detailed observations in fifty-eight classrooms. The researchers here showed that teachers tended to rely on one principal method of organizing their classes but, importantly, would shift their teaching style depending on what was happening in the classroom. Teachers would intelligently read the atmosphere and the needs of the class, at one moment becoming firmer, more didactic, and more formal, while at another allowing students more freedom to talk and explore ideas.

Teachers did, though, tend for most of the time to abide by one style in preference to another. Following observation, the researchers sifted teachers into categories they called 'group instructors', 'individual monitors', 'class enquirers', and 'style changers'. Children were also categorized into the styles *they* predominantly adopted: 'attention seekers', 'intermittent workers', 'solitary workers', and 'easy riders'. Interestingly, students in each of the categories, while they could be found with each of the teacher styles, tended to be particularly associated with one particular kind of teacher.

Take as an example the 'intermittent workers'. They are described by the authors as 'adept at carrying on their private exchanges with other pupils without drawing attention to themselves'. They were the pupils showing the lowest levels of contact with the teacher while showing the highest levels of contact with other pupils, spending 20 per cent of their time in activities coded as 'distraction'. These pupils were found least frequently among the 'class enquirers', or formal teachers, making it look as though these chalk-and-talk teachers had the answer when it came to classroom management.

Again, though, the interpretation shouldn't be that straightforward. Apart from questions about *what* children might be learning when they have their heads down, apparently studiously, there were more marked differences among the non-formal teachers than the formal ones, such that the very best teacher observed by the researchers—imaginative, inspiring, well organized, highly effective—was informal in her organization. Informal teaching could, however, seemingly go wrong more easily than formal teaching. Rather like the little girl with the curl in the nursery rhyme, when informal teaching was good it was very very good, but when it was bad it was horrid. In the hands of a run-of-the-mill teacher, formality seemed to offer a safer option.

Teachers think

What seems to me to come out of classroom research as it has become more sophisticated is a rather more complex picture than any conclusion that formal is better than progressive or vice versa. What emerges is a realization that teachers are not robots: they calculate and reflect, with, as one famous piece of research put it, their cultivation of an understanding of the 'ecology' of the classroom. They develop, as American classroom researcher Walter Doyle put it in the 1970s, 'with-it-ness'—having eyes in the back of their heads—and they are able to shift from one teaching style to another as necessary. Good teachers learn to multitask, attending to students' individual activities as well as managing the larger group. They respond to the class as well as leading it; they reflect on their successes and failures and they adapt.

Knowing that teaching is like this points the way to solving the mystery of why top-down efforts from governments to change schools so often fail. These efforts divert teachers from their experience and instincts, deliberately forcing them to bypass the teaching intelligence they have learned and nurtured. Those top-down efforts tell teachers: 'Do it this way.' But that doesn't work, as we have seen in both the USA and the UK over the last thirty years as efforts have been made by governments to impose this or that style of teaching or testing, this or that silver bullet curriculum, this or that form of 'what works'.

Thus, in the USA in 2001 Congress passed a new law—the 'No Child Left Behind' Act (NCLB)—which sought to increase accountability from schools through an array of measures, one of which instructed teachers on the kind of 'scientifically proven' practices they must adopt in their work. Only the 'best' methods of teaching were to be adopted, only 'scientifically proven' curricula to be followed. It sounds sensible enough, but the trouble is that commands of this kind wilfully bury the teacher's own personally developed skills. Teachers develop their own styles, suited to them and their students. If they are told to teach differently, in a way foreign to them or inappropriate to the needs of their students, this intelligence may be discarded. And the facts bear this out: the international statistics for the performance of American students for the period following the NCLB injunction show little if any improvement (as shown in Table 2).

Much the same is the case in the UK, where the last decade of the 20th century and the first of the 21st were characterized by imposition from on high of various strategies, such as the National Literacy Strategy. At first it looked as if these were working, but as is the case with so much innovation of this kind the effects rapidly fell away such that more mature evaluation shows no benefit from their introduction.

A renowned example of this genre of mistakes comes in the introduction of a method of teaching called Direct Instruction, a technique in which great hopes were invested in the USA in the 1970s and 1980s. Those hopes rested in a hyper-rational set of ideas about teaching and learning basic skills and the adoption of supposedly 'teacher-proof' methods. Its early use promised much. Later evaluation, however, as part of the huge Follow Through

Table 2: International test scores (PISA) for fifteen-year-olds in the United States, pre and post NCLB

Subject	Year	
	2000	2009
Reading	504	500
Mathematics	493	487
Science	499	502

project evaluation, indicated that the benefits attributed to it early on seemed to be due more to the generous resourcing assigned to it than to its specific pedagogic elements.

Even more worryingly, analysis over time indicated that any immediate benefits which might have accrued from the use of the technique were ultimately lost, and on leaving school those children who were part of a Direct Instruction curriculum were significantly more likely to have been involved in crime, were less well adjusted and engaged in fewer community activities than those who partook in traditional nursery activities at an earlier age. If there had been more trust in teachers' understanding of their craft, less credence may have been paid to the trite fixes that Direct Instruction and its ilk promised.

Such failures should not surprise us. These initiatives fail because they disable teachers: they prevent teachers acting and reacting as they see fit as reasoning professionals. They immobilize teachers, disconnecting them from their experience and their intelligence as professionals—substituting a set of routines and procedures for professional understanding and acumen.

Policymakers should perhaps learn more from the Finns, who avoid imposing 'teacher-proof' approaches on their schools. Instead, they cleave to their respect for the teacher's knowledge, skill, and professionalism. In Finland, teaching is a highly sought-after career; teachers are universally respected, paid well, and are all educated to Master's degree level. They are trusted to do a good job...and the trust pays off: even using the most formal measures of success, such as those employed in international comparison tables, the schools of the English-speaking countries lag well behind those of the Finns.

Chapter 4
Big ideas from the 20th century

The 20th century was a time of extraordinary change. Political and intellectual landscapes shifted; there was revolution and war, depression and boom. As the century began, science was uncovering new truths every year and in its slipstream the authority of the Church was fast drifting away. An intellectual climate was being created in which challenge to received ideas became accepted—expected, even. In the tumult, critique of established ideas and systems became the norm, and education was no exception to this rule: people asked questions more assertively about the purpose of school.

John Dewey and friends

All of this happened in education as there was a shift in the centre of gravity on educational thought from Europe to the USA. The European thought pioneers—Locke, Rousseau, Froebel—had done the spadework, but any challenge to received wisdom about education remained something of a fringe activity. Now, the changes of the 20th century created the conditions for John Dewey, a professor of philosophy first at the University of Michigan and ultimately at Columbia University, seriously to challenge accepted methods. He talked about the relationship of

4. John Dewey

education to democracy and he put this in the context of the way that schools and classrooms were organized.

One strand of Dewey's uniqueness comes from his status as a bit of a polymath. He did not restrict himself to one branch of academic activity, being one of those people who emerge from time to time who manage to transcend disciplinary boundaries. Not only was he a philosopher and a psychologist, he was also an educator and a political theorist, and, more than this, he adroitly connected the Big Ideas of each field. In philosophy he stressed the need for a pragmatic (that is to say, a purposeful, useful) turn;

in psychology he emphasized the need to consider the social environment of the learner. While it is his contributions to education for which he is best known, in all that he did his commitment to democracy was pivotal, a commitment which makes his thinking resonate with that of Locke and Rousseau centuries before him.

Though prolific, Dewey's writing is mixed in quality. It can be laboured and repetitive, and what it lacks in fluency it doesn't always make up for in clarity. Nor, sadly, was his opacity as a writer compensated for by his spoken delivery. The 1928 *Time* article about Dewey's visit to China describes his delivery as 'monotonous, halting, full of long pauses'.

But never mind: reading him is well worth the effort, for while his prose is often awkward or contrived, it contains an abundance of riches. He asks, for example, in *Experience and Education*: 'How many students...were rendered callous to ideas, and how many lost the impetus to learn because of the way in which learning was experienced by them?...How many came to associate books with dull drudgery?' (pp 26–7)

In an echo of John Locke 200 years before, Dewey championed the child as an instinctive scientist. He says in the preface to *How We Think*: 'the native and unspoiled attitude of childhood, marked by ardent curiosity, fertile imagination, and love of experimental inquiry, is near, very near, to the attitude of the scientific mind'. He makes the point that the scientific way of solving problems lies not in some special set of tools and methods, but rather in a refinement of trial-and-error thinking. Learning to think is all about what another 20th-century philosopher, Karl Popper, came later to call 'conjectures and refutations'. Everyday problem solving, suggested Dewey (and Popper), comprises a process a bit like going into a coconut shy: you put ideas up and you do your best to knock them down again; you shouldn't just accept the first idea or explanation you think of, or the first idea which is presented to you. Try to topple it: only if an idea survives the onslaught of intelligent interrogation is it worthy of provisional acceptance.

This implies teaching children to be critical, which is of course a lot harder than teaching them to accept what you say without question. The latter, easier though it is, is destructive of education: 'Sheer imitation, dictation of steps to be taken, mechanical drill, may give results most quickly and yet strengthen traits likely to be fatal to reflective power' (p 51). In fact, teaching is about the 'development of curiosity, suggestion, and habits of exploring and testing' (pp 45–6).

He draws a distinction in *How We Think* between *belief* and *reflective thought*. He says: 'a belief is accepted with slight or almost no attempt to state the grounds that support it. In other cases, the ground or basis for a belief is deliberately sought and its adequacy to support the belief examined. This process is called reflective thought; it alone is truly educative in value' (p 1). For Dewey, reflective thinking is at the centre of education: education isn't about learning facts—it's about being sceptical and critical.

This emphasis on criticality is crucial: it's the nub of Dewey's philosophy of education. Like Locke back in the 17th century, Dewey was stressing the need for the cultivation of critical thinking for the making of a fair, open-minded citizenry—one which is able to think independently to contest bad ideas and question leaders. And it is raised again and again in discourse about education. The celebrated educators Neil Postman and Charles Weingartner continue in Dewey's tradition by drawing on Ernest Hemingway's idea of the 'crap detector' to encapsulate the notion of critical awareness. Critical awareness, or crap detection, they suggest, could be said to be what education is all about. They put it like this:

> One way of looking at the history of the human group is that it has
> been a continuing struggle against the veneration of 'crap'. Our

intellectual history is a chronicle of the anguish and suffering of
men who tried to help their contemporaries see that some part of
their fondest beliefs were misconceptions, faulty assumptions,
superstitions and even outright lies. The mileposts along the road of
our intellectual development signal those points at which some
person developed a new perspective, a new meaning, or a new
metaphor. We have in mind a new education that would set out to
cultivate just such people—experts at 'crap detecting'.

Dewey went on to draw a distinction between information and
knowledge, noting that schools concentrate on the former at the
expense of the latter. 'Covering the ground' is the primary
necessity; the nurture of mind a bad second (p 52). And in a
comment on the nature of education as promoted by politicians,
which could quite easily have been written today, let alone a
hundred years ago, he speaks of the damage done to children's
learning by testing 'success' through easily audited indicators of
one kind or another:

> There is no great difficulty in understanding why this ideal
> [i.e. testing] has such vogue. The large number of pupils to be dealt
> with, and the tendency of parents and school authorities to demand
> speedy and tangible evidence of progress, conspire to give it
> currency. (pp 53–4)

Dewey's concern for the relationship between education and
democracy made the point that democracy is not just a form of
government—it is, rather, 'a mode of associated living, a conjoint
communicated experience' (1916: 101). A good society was for
Dewey an open society where people related on equal terms and
all benefited from the work that they devoted to society. A school
should be a place where the good society is fostered and
epitomized: people should intermingle irrespective of background
or ability. This was essential for the democratic society. Dewey's
thought here provided one of the foundation stones for the
dismantling of the selective system in the UK in the 1960s and

1970s and the introduction of the comprehensive schools to replace selective secondary schools.

Dewey became a professor at Columbia's Teachers College, which, the great American educator Lawrence Cremin noted, educated 'a substantial percentage of the articulate leaders of American education'. Professors there between 1918 and 1940, he noted, exercised 'a prodigious influence on educational theory and practice' (1961: 220). Dewey's disciple and successor in that post, William Kilpatrick, continued the tradition. Dewey's protégé noted that schools should produce 'better citizens, alert, able to think and act, too intelligently critical to be easily hoodwinked either by politicians or patent-medicines, self-reliant, ready of adaptation to the new social conditions that impend' (pp 326–7).

Plowden the progressive

In the USA, then, new generations of teachers were being schooled in Dewey's ideas during the interwar years. A similar kind of movement was happening in Europe, where Dewey was also having an impact, but where there was also the influence from some important thinkers with their experimental schools— figures such as A.S. Neill and Maria Montessori. And out of all of this—out of all the questioning from the progressives—there came in Britain at the cusp of the 1920s and 1930s the Board of Education's reports on a range of educational topics under the chairmanship of Sir William Hadow. Apart from anything else, these led to the formal separation of two stages of schooling with a break at age eleven. Perhaps the most influential of Hadow's reports was the Report of the Consultative Committee on the Primary School. It made some remarkably forward-looking comments, such as this:

> Is their curriculum humane and realistic, unencumbered by the
> dead wood of a formal tradition, quickened by inquiry and
> experiment, and inspired, not by an attachment to conventional

orthodoxies, but by a vivid appreciation of the needs and possibilities of the children themselves? Are their methods of organisation and the character of their equipment, the scale on which they are staffed, and the lines on which their education is planned, of a kind best calculated to encourage individual work and persistent practical activity among pupils, initiative and originality among teachers, and to foster in both the spirit which leaves the beaten path and strikes fearlessly into new fields, which is the soul of education?

Hadow Report, pp xiii–xiv

It continued that the curriculum 'must be vivid, realistic, a stream in motion, not a stagnant pool'. Apart from its substance, what is remarkable about the Hadow Report is the allure of the prose. It's not written in the dull officialese of today's official reports and documents, which seem to spend more time deliberating on procedures than they do reflecting on pedagogy. There is poetry and rhetoric in Hadow, as if the reader is ready and waiting to be persuaded of the benefits of a new kind of education.

But the rhetoric and optimism in Hadow's writing should not obscure the fact that this was the 1930s. These were hard times: the Depression was taking its toll on confidence and neither public nor politicians were ready for a document that told them that the needs of the world of work were secondary to the flowering of the child's imagination. Imagination? Snort: who needs it? Hitler was just over the water. The ground had been prepared, though, and despite the scepticism about the progressive position (scepticism that continues to this day), by the end of the Second World War a new generation of teachers was ready for something new—something that embodied the Hadow principles. In the UK, it is the Plowden Report of the 1960s that is generally credited with (or blamed for, depending on which way you look at it) the more systematic introduction of progressive ideas. It is clear, though, that it was the Hadow committee which had done the spadework.

Plowden is a fascinating document. The membership of the committee on its own has a distinctly sixties-ish and even Pythonesque flavour about it. Look at the list of committee members and you will find that first in the dramatis personae was the world-famous logical positivist philosopher Sir A.J. 'Freddie' Ayer (Wykeham Professor of Logic at the University of Oxford). While his talents in philosophy were surely undisputed, his qualifications for advising on the state's education of small children were less conspicuous. With his mother a Citroën heiress and his father a financier for the Rothschilds, his family clearly hadn't wanted for very much and with his own education at Eton, the Guards, and Oxford he probably had not been inconvenienced too much by contact with the great unwashed during his own formative years. Alongside him there sat Mrs M. Bannister, who, in echoes of Dame Edna, was described as 'Housewife and Parent', and, beyond them, the improbable-sounding Brigadier L.L. Thwaytes, together with Lady Plowden herself and eighteen others.

It was a strange mix for the civil servants to concoct, bearing signs both of respect for class and the beginnings of consciousness about its legacy. What is clear, though, is that its members were not the battle-hardened Marxists whom contemporary detractors from Plowden seem to imagine when they attack the report and its supposed effects in the degradation of morals, learning, and life in general. Given the committee's constitution, it's all the more remarkable that it produced probably the single strongest official impetus for progressive education in the 20th century anywhere in the world.

Lady Plowden's report noted that any changes that had taken place in schools between 1900 and the 1960s had been unplanned and uncoordinated—excusably, perhaps, given that there had been two catastrophic world wars sandwiching a ruinous global depression over precisely that period: people had had their minds occupied by matters a tad more sombre than the *pensées* of

Jean-Jacques Rousseau. Now, though, said Plowden, was the time for change. The committee asked: 'Has "finding out" proved to be better than "being told"? Have methods been worked out through which discovery can be stimulated and guided, and children develop from it a coherent body of knowledge? Has the emphasis which the Hadow Report placed on individual progress been justified by its results?' (p 2).

It sought to find the answers to these questions. The committee visited primary schools in many countries: Denmark, France, Sweden, Poland, the USA, and the USSR. It noted that the concerns were the same everywhere: the curriculum, teaching methods, how to provide for children of differing abilities, how to help most effectively children from 'poor circumstances'.

If you read the Plowden Report after reading the Hadow Report you'll see something rather interesting added to Hadow's common sense and straightforward philosophy about the importance of allowing children to discover and to nurture growth and learning as they discover. It is possible to detect in the 1967 document a new kind of expertism coming in—expertism from the 'ologies': psychology and sociology—with reference to the intellectual growth of the child, children's learning, and their place in society. There's talk of 'skills' and 'development'—new words when it came to education—and with this talk we can see psychology, especially, beginning to leave its imprint more firmly.

The committee recognized this itself, and explicitly contrasted two prominent groups of psychologists who may have had something to offer the education debate. The first group comprised psychologists in the behavioural school, with figures such as B.F. Skinner and Ivan Pavlov. We would nowadays probably call the second group 'constructivist' or 'cognitive' or 'sociocultural' psychologists, though the committee did not venture to name them as such. This latter school (or schools) they took to be associated with psychologists such as the British Susan Isaacs, the

Russian Alexander Luria, the American Jerome Bruner, and the Swiss Jean Piaget.

Plowden preferred these latter constructivists to the behaviourists as providing a frame for thinking about education. The behaviourists, the committee concluded, had too narrow a view of learning, and one which, if used, would restrict opportunities for children's cognitive growth. The favoured constructivists were more disparate in their views on learning and development, though we can broadly align them with the thinking of the progressive pioneers. Susan Isaacs, especially, was close to Locke and Rousseau in the pre-eminence she accorded to play in the development of the young person's capacity for learning. She looks rather like the love child of Locke and Rousseau (if we allow for some gender reconstruction), in that she has an especially interesting view of play as involving a perpetual form of experimentation by the child.

Luria—and other Russian psychologists such as Lev Vygotsky (whom Plowden strangely doesn't mention)—also stressed the importance of play in learning, but put this especially into the context of language and social connection: language is the tool for thought while social intercourse is the means by which it is developed—not a new idea, of course, but one which now had the official endorsement of psychology as one of the new 'social sciences': so it was now officially sanctioned by science. Bruner and Piaget concentrated more on the ways that children actually think and how thinking develops. I'll look at these characters in more detail in Chapter 5.

These psychologists were influential for European education in the middle of the 20th century, but the mood was changing in the USA too. There, though, in America, the provenance of the change in mood was rather different. The post-war period and the sixties had brought with them a yearning for greater freedoms and for self-expression, as had been the case in Europe, but for Americans individual rights and equality of opportunity took centre stage

"190 divided by two..."

5. The work of psychologists such as Piaget and Bruner suggested that we need to understand the ways children think in order to teach them

more than had been the case in Europe, and the arguments were expressed more in demands for equality—not least those centred around ethnicity, gender, and, less prominently, disability. In all of this came a questioning of authority and of the institutions which were rooted in that authority. School itself, as an institution, was examined in detail.

John Holt: jewels from the classroom

Ultimately more influential in the USA, and later in Europe, was one extraordinary figure, who was neither an academic educator nor a developmental psychologist. This was John Holt, a Boston teacher. He began his bestselling book *How Children Fail* in 1964 with words from the psychologist William Hull: 'If we taught children to speak, they'd never learn.' He went on to explain what Hull had meant by this: that teaching, by instilling boredom or anxiety (or both), can destroy a child's natural ability to learn, and if we tried to teach children to speak in the way that we try to teach them to read, they'd never learn. They would, he said, get discouraged, humiliated, confused, and angry. They'd become mute.

With some beautiful insights, Holt said what many knew already instinctively about school, merely by having passed through it themselves. His method was to reflect on his own experience of teaching in his Boston classroom, by giving vignettes—diary entries of his work with children. He mused on the things children said and did in response to his questions, and he revealed by so doing that they seemed to be entering a kind of other-world when in the classroom. It was almost as if, when in class, nine-tenths of their brains were taken over by some process which had nothing to do with the task in hand and everything to do with pleasing the teacher, or avoiding looking stupid, or both. These latter became the principal objectives of the pupil. Take this passage, which is one of Holt's diary entries, dated 22 April 1960, describing a girl's travails with the 7 times table. She had made some simple mistakes that showed that she had not been thinking at all about the task:

> I thought if I could get her to think about what she had written, she would see that some of her answers were more reasonable than others, and thus the beginnings of an error-noticing, nonsense-eliminating device might take root in her mind. I gave her all three

papers, and asked her, since they did not agree, to compare her answers, check with a ✓ those she felt sure were right, with an X those she felt sure were wrong, and with a ? those she wasn't sure of one way or the other. A moment later I got one of the most unpleasant surprises of my teaching career. She handed me her corrected paper, with 7 times 1 marked right, and *all other answers* marked wrong. This poor child has been defeated and destroyed by school. Years of drill, practice, explanation, and testing—the whole process we call education—have done nothing for her except help to knock her loose from what common sense she might have had to start with. (p 251)

All teachers have met this girl. Actually, I understate the problem: all teachers meet her, and many others like her, every day of their working lives. Her demeanour, if, in its extreme, is not quite the norm, is nevertheless ubiquitous. Holt said that children lose their innate and extraordinary capacity for learning because of what is done in schools. He continues (in the conclusion): 'we make them afraid to gamble, afraid to experiment, afraid to try the difficult and the unknown'. It's interesting that contemporary commentators say much the same about school today. In *What's the Point of School?* Guy Claxton notes that, rather than becoming braver and bolder, children in fact become more docile and fragile in the face of difficulty. 'They learn,' he says, 'to think narrowly rather than broadly...to be frightened of uncertainty and the risk of error that accompanies it.'

Holt's book is less widely read now than it was in its heyday, when it sold well over one million copies. In the main, teachers cheered it even though it was critical of their work. They shouted 'Yes!' when reading it not just because of its remarkable insights about children's learning and behaviour at school, but also because it revealed the enormity of the task teachers face. They have to operate a rusty machine while being asked to churn out results and 'improved standards' with this contraption. Holt put his finger on this without using psychological jargon and without

HOW CHILDREN FAIL

'To anyone who deals with children and cares about children, it cannot be too highly recommended' – *The New York Times*

JOHN HOLT

6. The cover of John Holt's groundbreaking *How Children Fail*

sentimentality. I see his book as one of the most important on education in the 20th century.

For Americans, the post-war years had brought not just mistrust in authority and a confidence to question its edicts but also a world-leading role in fighting a Cold War. This was accompanied, for many, by a fear bordering on paranoia about the threat of communism, and there was a dread about losing the technology race with the USSR. Iconic in this atmosphere of anxiety was the Soviets' launch of Sputnik in 1957, to most of the world's awe but to America's embarrassment. The ensuing soul searching included self-doubt about educational systems and the amount invested in particular in science and technology. The success of the Soviet Sputnik was accompanied also by discussion not just about content—not just about the stuff of science education—but about the creativity and inventiveness fostered in youngsters by schools. Were schools snuffing out imagination, ingenuity, resourcefulness? Was that why the communists were forging ahead?

This question about inventiveness and creativity linked with the issues that John Holt had been raising. So the command to schools—the invective about education—was, perhaps as ever, Janus-like: the injunction was to teach more and get better results, but to get kids to be imaginative and creative at the same time. They had to learn the facts of science, but they shouldn't have original thinking squeezed from them in the process. It was the formal versus progressive controversy in a nutshell.

The neoliberal turn

If the suffusion of progressive thinking into the ideas of psychology set the direction and shape of education for most of the 20th century, the final part of the century saw an influence from an entirely unfamiliar place make its mark. That influence came from politics and economics more than it came from education. Before the final quarter of the century politics and education had rarely had much to do with each other, except insofar as politicians and policymakers did their best to garner and to listen to informed opinion and to respond, as had been the case with various committees' advice to the government in the UK. It had been, as sociologist of education Stephen Ball has put it, a 'settlement' about education policy: politicians and educators had rubbed along nicely.

But now, in the last part of the century, government took its own robust view about the way that education should be organized. On both sides of the Atlantic there was a new political awakening, and politically inspired changes affected the way that education would develop for the next thirty years—until the present day, in fact.

Where did this new urge for agenda setting come from? Ironically, in the UK at least, in part it had been born of the settlement itself—of governments *listening* to the advice they received in reports but then failing to *act* effectively. They knew how to analyse what was being done *wrong*, but they didn't put nearly as much thought, activity, or money into how to do it *right*. Thus, the dismantling of the selective system and the introduction of comprehensive schools was, as Stephen Ball put it, 'piecemeal and incoherent' (p 71). There was, he suggests, 'little evidence of political will for thoroughgoing change'.

The result was a backlash against the comprehensive schools, which had been introduced with such little forethought. The settlement was abandoned as a strange kind of counterculture emerged among politicians—counter to the settlement, that is. Widely publicized pamphlets such as the *Black Papers* argued for a return to the selective system, and stories of egregiously failing schools such as Risinghill and William Tyndale appeared in the newspaper headlines. Across the political spectrum there was consensus that the problems which seemed to be emerging in schools were the fault of 'poor teachers, weak head-teachers . . . and modern teaching methods' as the UK Labour government's Secretary of State for Education Shirley Williams put it in 1977. Such comments were matched in the USA with *A Nation at Risk?*, the Reagan administration's analysis of what was supposedly going wrong in schools, which bemoaned the 'rising tide of mediocrity'.

All of this coincided with ideas which were emerging out of a new economic model that had its intellectual seed in the Chicago School of economics of the 1920s and 1930s: neoliberalism, a brand of economics that put markets and individual choice at the core of economic success. Though neoliberalism had lain dormant for a time, it had gained credibility following a powerful post-war consumerism, which had made the consumer the hero, the driving force in effecting change in the economic environment. The neoliberal turn gathered speed in the early 1980s, happening alongside the ramping up of the Cold War rhetoric that had emerged as part of the Thatcher–Reagan alliance. There was an invigorated narrative about the failure of state-run systems and a focus on the contrasting economic models in use on either side of the Iron Curtain.

Following the confidence that accompanied *glasnost, perestroika* and the fall of the Berlin Wall came a new certainty from the West that it had the right economic model—the big questions about the distribution of resources had, it seemed, been resolved. Francis Fukuyama even talked about *The End of History*—the 'end' being in the triumph of liberal democracy in politics working through the mechanism of free markets in economic life. *Choice* was the watchword: people would choose how they wanted to be governed and they would choose the goods and the services they wanted via the market.

Neoliberalism was bound up with this new thinking and as the education settlement was challenged across continents, people began to take an interest particularly in the ideas of one of the architects of neoliberalism, the economist Milton Friedman, and especially in his ideas on education. Back in 1955 Friedman had turned his attention to education and written *The Role of Government in Education*. Education intrigued him because of its strange and, for the market model, rather irritating position in the marketplace. It didn't quite fit into a neat demand-and-supply framework with choice at the centre.

There was, Friedman realized, anomalously for the new economic model and the primacy it gave to consumer choice, a need for state funding of schools. This was because the whole of society benefits from individuals' education. If Jo gets educated, and pays for her own education, I benefit in all sorts of ways—from her enhanced civic awareness, her improved productivity, and so on... even though I don't pay for Jo's education. I benefit in the way I wouldn't if Jo just bought a vacuum cleaner. Friedman called such benefits 'neighbourhood effects'—the benefits that come from services that aren't paid for. Because of these neighbourhood effects government is justified, he said, in taxing to provide for these unusual good-for-everyone services—notably education.

His deliberations on neighbourhood effects made Friedman ask where they left the idea of *choice*. If government had to provide schools through taxation, where did this leave the wisdom of the market? Parents knew what they wanted for their children—they knew what was best, not government—but government was doing the choosing for them.

He resolved the conundrum of neighbourhood effects by coming up with the idea of creating market conditions in the state-funded system. If such conditions could be created, he argued, we would have the best of both worlds: state funding, but with parent choice. He suggested that parents should therefore be issued with vouchers by the government with which they could 'buy' a school place at whichever school they wished—state, private, religious, whatever. If spent at a private school, the voucher could be topped up with the parents' own money to the level of the school's fees.

But the voucher idea wasn't latched on to enthusiastically by governments (though it has been tried in some places across the world, the USA and Sweden among them) mainly because it was seen as a means of insidiously enabling various kinds of unwelcome segregation to prosper. I should note here that segregation in the USA meant more than simply separation by ability—the kind of separation and segregation I have been discussing so far. Before proceeding with the story of the neoliberal turn, I need to make a short diversion to say a little more about it.

Segregation

Until the 1950s and 1960s, certain American states had racially segregated their schools. This segregation was undone, in theory at least, by the US Supreme Court in 1954 with the case of *Brown et al. v. Board of Education of Topeka et al.* In his summing up on this case Chief Justice Warren, on behalf of the Supreme Court, rejected the segregation that was occurring in some states' schools: 'We conclude that, in the field of public education, the doctrine of "separate but equal" has no place. Separate educational facilities are inherently unequal.'

It's hardly believable that it was necessary for a court in the USA to assert this only half a century ago, but it's testament perhaps to the spirit of those times that Chief Justice Warren's comments did not make the problem go away. Attempts by state legislatures to oppose the law continued, culminating in the segregated University of Mississippi in 1962 refusing access to an African American, James Meredith. The Mississippi governor, Ross Barnett, insisted that 'No school will be integrated in Mississippi while I am your Governor,' resulting in the Attorney General of the time, Robert Kennedy, ordering marshals to escort James Meredith onto the campus. The ensuing rioting, during which white students and others hurled rocks at marshals, led, by presidential order, to the dispatch of troops to the university to quell the riot and enforce Meredith's attendance.

Abandoned now, segregation of students into different schools by race has presented the starkest and most egregiously insulting kind of separation, but it has been an abiding impulse in schools and school systems to separate one group from another. This exists in strong and weak forms. The strong and explicit form continues to exist in special education, where those who cannot or will not fit into the envelopes provided by mainstream schools are sent to special schools, where a different experience is provided—an experience usually that exists in an abbreviated curriculum and an abnormal social experience. It exists in its weak form in more finely graded differentiations based on youngsters' attainment, a practice that goes under various names: streaming, setting, banding. Harvard academic Martha Minow concludes from a major review of the research that via these means—'renewed racial segregation through academic tracking, special education assignments, and students' own divisions in lunch tables and cliques'—racial segregation is as common as ever, half a century after the *Brown* judgment.

Quasi-markets, competition, and testing

I've noted these facts about segregation because they are, strangely, at the heart of both the desire for choice and the anxieties about its effects. If the presidential intervention put paid to formal attempts to segregate by 'race', the legacy of segregation hung on in informal attempts to select and segregate. This is where, to return to Milton Friedman's ideas about vouchers, fear about the extent to which vouchers might enable racial segregation to happen by the back door meant that his ideas were, in most places, treated with caution. There was, you can probably see, ambivalence about choice: many politicians wanted to allow choice, but they didn't want it to proliferate unchecked.

Friedman had tried to provide for marketization in education with the impracticable vouchers, but toward the end of the century a solution was found which seemingly circumvented the problems of segregation which vouchers had raised. The solution with which policymakers emerged existed in various forms of reorganization, most notably in the establishment of a new kind of artificial market, a quasi-market, within state-run systems. In this quasi-market there would be customers, or 'purchasers'—the parents with their children; and there would be 'providers'—the schools. As parents chose where they wanted their children to go to school, packets of money would more conspicuously accompany each child, and the more popular schools would receive these packets of money and thrive, while the unpopular ones would lose income as customers drifted away.

The logic of the market ideology dictated that its planners should construct the quasi-market so that it resembled as far as possible an actual market. So, given that a good market needs as much choice as possible to be available to purchasers, more choice could surely be supplied by enabling a broader range of schools to emerge, all working in different ways, offering different curricular or pastoral specialities. We see this now operationalized in the emergence of academies, free schools, and specialist colleges in the UK, and charter schools and magnet schools in the USA. The power of regularizing go-betweens, such as local government, is deliberately trimmed down as schools are freed from various rules and statutory responsibilities, such as the responsibility to follow the National Curriculum in the UK academies. No longer would these go-betweens have any oversight of decisions about where children (and therefore their packets of money) were directed. Diversity and parent choice are thus increased as schools emerge and disappear in an increasingly free market, unfettered by considerations for local planning or regulation. (This is sometimes called a 'supply-side solution'—one that solves problems by enabling supply, in this case supply of schools, to increase.)

Classical economics tells us also that markets need customers to be supplied with as much information as possible about the choices they are making. The quasi-market was thus stimulated by the provision of that information: published test results and school inspection reports would tell parents how each school was faring compared to other schools.

We are currently living through the marketization revolution of education, and like any contemporary phenomenon it is difficult to see the wood for the trees and appreciate its ultimate significance. Will it be bang or whimper? My own view is that the kind of market notionally being introduced is unlikely ever actually to operate as a real market, such as one in which groceries are bought and sold, for three main reasons...

- When provided with the information that their breakfast cereal provides too little fibre in the diet, consumers can easily make a change to another. But no such change is easy, or even possible, in the schools quasi-market, where parents, if dissatisfied, will be loath to switch a child's school, for a plethora of reasons: friends, distance, the damaging effects of a change of curriculum, and so on.

- A market should be characterized by a wide variety of choice but such variety is restricted by the critical mass needed to support a viable school with a broad curriculum: it simply will not be possible, especially in rural and suburban areas, for enough schools to emerge within travelling distance to provide realistic choice.

- The information provided on which choice is notionally to be made provides little fine-grain detail and is weighted towards test results. As we have seen, these results can give a false impression of the quality of education on offer in a school.

The idea of 'choice' in a market of schools therefore seems a misnomer, since that choice is made at a single point in time among very few alternatives with scant information about how to make the choice, and next to no possibility of reversing it.

The market will, again in the language of economics, always be distorted because of imperfect competition which is both inbuilt and endemic: there is both oligopoly (few 'sellers' in the form of schools in any one locale) and the existence of a form of monopsony, in which certain 'buyers' (the parents of more able children, for example) are able to dictate terms to the sellers (the schools). In these circumstances, schools will face persistent pressure to become more selective. When Lord Adonis, a UK education minister, told private school headteachers that 'It is your educational DNA we are seeking' in establishing the reform of a freed-up market of state schools, he ignored the fact that it was *selection* that was at the core of this DNA. As John Claughton, the Chief Master of the prestigious private King Edward's School in Birmingham, aptly put it in response:

> [T]here is the word that dare not speak its name: selection. The majority of independent schools proceed by academic selection and they do that because they believe that it is fundamental to their success. So schools had every right to wonder whether this particular DNA was really going to be that useful.

There are important after-effects which emerge from the addition of market-type characteristics to education, most notably those that appear after the provision of information in the 'market' by testing and the publication of test results. This imposes such an unprecedentedly heavy test load on schools that the curriculum itself is distorted, with teaching and the judgements made by staff in schools about educational outcomes all bending to the pressure of achieving top results. The pressure is not just on staff, but on the children themselves.

How should we review the marketization story of the past thirty years? Perhaps most significantly, there is little or no evidence for the success of the market-orientated changes that have been introduced. In the USA, where charter schools have been operating since the early 1990s, evaluations of their performance are wholly inconclusive, with some substantial research indicating that charter schools are, in the main, doing worse rather than better than their unreformed public school counterparts. The findings of research in the UK about the more recently established academies are similarly inconclusive.

The current marketization of education is sometimes described as 'radical' reform. It is certainly introducing some serious change—the destabilization of the teaching profession and the fixation with testing among them—and these are documented in detail by Diane Ravitch in her magisterial review, *The death and life of the great American school system: How testing and choice are undermining education.* (Ravitch, it is important to say, is no Marxist. She initially supported certain of the 'reforms' and advised various US administrations at the highest level.) It is difficult, however, to see how 'reform', radical or otherwise, is being induced. Reform will surely come only with some serious questions being asked about what we want from schools in today's world—what we expect education to be. I address some of these questions in Chapter 7.

Finally, can the 'invisible hand' of the market be entrusted with the job of guiding reform in an area as complex as education? Even in purely instrumental terms markets are not always reliable, as we have dramatically witnessed from their unregulated performance recently in the banking arena. Henry Ford, so famously successful in responding to consumer demand (and perhaps a more practically minded economist than Milton Friedman), put the case well in averring that he could never have relied on consumers for determining the direction of his car-making plans: 'If I'd asked my customers what they wanted, they'd have said a faster horse,' noted Ford. People want what they already know about.

The danger is that engineering a market in education may result in nothing but the construction of a shabby facsimile of the private education system—wanting in its nature to attract those youngsters who are the most receptive to formal education, and wanting to exclude the most difficult to teach. As Harvard political philosopher Michael Sandel asks: 'are there certain moral and civic goods that markets do not honour?'

Chapter 5
Analysts and theorists: what did they ever do for us?

Time-travelling Martian anthropologists beamed from a school in 1900 to another in 2000 would be certain that they had materialized in the same kind of institution. Each establishment would contain classrooms, teachers standing in front of pupils, tables, desks, timetables. For the 2000 class, though, our Martian friends would have jotted down some big changes in their notebooks: smaller classes with more diversity in the pupil population; less regimentation; less didactic teaching.

How and why did these changes happen? Increasing wealth, major shifts in demography, and an opening up of society to become less in thrall to authority were of course prime movers. And, as we have seen, changes had occurred as a consequence of the commentary of social reformers such as Charles Dickens on the patent absurdity and routine cruelty of some of education's processes. Change came also from the analyses of a new class of professional educators such as Dewey.

Significantly, though, changes in the style of school—in the ways that teachers taught—came from a new genre of observers and analysts: the social scientists. They proffered new insights on learning, teaching, and how schools worked. The offering of these new analysts, though, has been mixed: while the new understandings of social science made for welcome reform in many ways, in other ways the contribution has proved more beguiling than productive. Because social science isn't quite the same as natural science—for the refutation of bad or silly ideas can never be quite as clear cut—some wild goose chases have been pursued in the quest for an understanding of learning and the ways in which it happens in schools. In this chapter I'll look at some of the avenues that have been followed in response to the ideas and the research of the new analysts.

Psychology's rise

Born at the end of the 19th century, the infant science of psychology expanded rapidly between the wars and during that time psychologists raised questions about how children grew as thinkers. They asked, for example, if there were different stages through which children travelled in their development of sophisticated, adult thinking. Did children think differently from adults—not just more naively, but actually *differently*, using a different kind of mental architecture from adults? The answers to these questions clearly ought to have important consequences for teachers, for if children reasoned and learned differently, teachers should—if their teaching was going to have an impact—adapt the ways that they taught, accommodating the learning needs of the child. By the middle of the 20th century there were, broadly speaking, three theories about these questions, each different in the way that it conceived of learning and in the conclusions that it drew about the ways that teachers should teach.

The first was that of the Swiss psychologist Jean Piaget. Using his own children as subjects in his natural experiments, he figured— both from these observations and from work he had been doing on intelligence testing—that children did indeed think differently from adults. Young children would regularly and consistently give wrong answers to certain kinds of question. For example, if the water from a tall jar were to be poured into a shorter, fatter jar, young children, when asked, would say that the taller jar had contained more water.

Piaget argued from these observations that children pass through different stages of thinking: first, a sensorimotor stage, between birth and about two years of age, when movement and senses are everything, though here the child will learn important skills such as 'object permanence', or the ability to realize that objects continue to exist even when we can't see them. Then, he said, there was a preoperational stage from about two years old to about seven years old when children are highly egocentric, not really being able to understand how the world looks to others. Following this was a concrete operations stage, from seven to eleven, and finally a formal operations stage from around eleven upwards when abstract and logical thought would develop. Each stage was characterized by profound differences in the kinds of thinking with which children would be able to cope. For example, Piaget called children's eventual ability to work out that the two jars in the jar task held identical amounts of water, the ability to *conserve* (that is to say, to 'hold in their heads' the amount in the first jar as it was poured to a different place) and this came at the concrete operations stage, between seven and eleven, but not before.

Piagetian theory had an important corollary for teaching. It suggested a certain fixity in the way that thinking develops, with its view that the stages through which children passed were genetically determined and unvarying. It cautioned that children had to pass through these stages in sequence; if a stage hadn't been traversed, then children would not be able to cope with the concepts characteristic of the next stage: they would not have the mental dexterity to cope with more complex ideas. It thus led, most seriously, to the idea of *readiness*: that children needed to be *ready* to cope with certain kinds of learning and teaching. They shouldn't be taught to read too soon, for example, or they would become bored, confused, or even anxious about learning.

7. Piaget's *object permanence* described children's ability to know that an object existed when it could no longer be seen

Accurate though that last point is—children can indeed become dispirited and anxious if pushed too hard—in many ways, Piaget's ideas didn't ring true. Given the right circumstances, young children do sometimes seem able to perform some quite heavy-duty feats of logic: we're often delighted by the things children are able to work out, especially if they are given help from an interested adult.

If you reflect on the kind of learning that children develop in real life, you'll realize that this adult assistance is highly relevant. So it was inappropriate, critics of Piaget said, for the great developmental psychologist to base his theory about children's learning on a set of observations which failed to take account of such help. In fact, we really ought to consider very seriously the help children receive in building their models for thinking. Learning is rarely a lone pursuit to be deliberated over anxiously by the unaided child, and children's behaviour in such solitary situations tells us little about the ways that they think and learn.

Challenges to Piaget's ideas came, most notably, from the work of the Oxford psychologist Peter Bryant in the 1970s. His research, alongside that of a range of others across the world, showed that children could indeed work beyond their supposed Piagetian cognitive stage as long as they were given the right help and the right circumstances. Their confusion with the jar task, for example, may simply have been a confusion about the word 'more'—did it, for the child, just mean 'taller'? If the task were to be explained to them fully, they could answer appropriately.

For many educators these challenges came as a relief. Piagetian orthodoxy was felt by many teachers to imply that development rested more on simple biological growth than it did on the work of the teacher. Although Bryant happily conceded that one side of Piaget's theory had been helpful (in showing that children *build* a mental world for themselves, rather than having one delivered to them), he cautioned that 'there can be no question that the implications of Piaget's theories about children's logical skills are, as far as teachers are concerned, restrictive and negative' (p 257).

Although it had these 'restrictive and negative' implications, Piaget's work had a great deal of influence on the education of teachers because of the consequences that the staged view of development seemed to imply for the structuring and sequencing of teaching. From the 1950s until the end of the 20th century, despite the challenges to its validity, it took a central place in the theory of education taught to many teachers in training: it was taken to be relevant to a wide range of topics from the teaching of reading to the teaching of science.

Unfortunately, in this education of teachers, Piaget's contribution to our understanding of children's thinking has focused on his developmental stages and how children pass (or don't pass) through them, to the extent that his main message has been relatively disregarded. That important message, rather at variance with the biological determinism of the stages, was about young children building their own mental models—*constructing* their own worlds through their experience. Because of this emphasis on the individual construction of the world, his approach has come to be known as *constructivism*.

This idea about *constructing* a mental world—the core, really, of Piaget's highly significant contribution, if we forget his

74

unfortunate stages—leads us to the 20th century's second stream of psychological thought, the theory of the 'social constructivists', notably Lev Vygotsky and Jerome Bruner. Vygotsky was a psychologist working in the pre-war Soviet Union; Bruner is a post-war Harvard psychologist. They, and their situations, couldn't have been more different. But, working in strikingly different places and at different times, they said similar things.

As with Piaget, the emphasis of Vygotsky and Bruner was on the way children constructed their own models for thinking, but they saw this construction happening in a markedly different way from the Swiss psychologist. Both stressed the importance of language in learning and this in itself was new and a contrast with Piaget. An even more important contrast, though, was that both placed great store on the kind of help that a child has from a mentor, such as a parent or teacher. Bruner came up with the analogy of parents and teachers *scaffolding* the new skills that the child was learning, by providing support and guidance to get to the next point. Vygotsky gave educators the notion of the rather clumsily named *zone of proximal development*—the idea that there is an area of activity which is just a little bit beyond what a child can already do: it is what they can do with help. It is this area on which teaching should concentrate.

You might ask if all of this isn't a bit obvious. Isn't it self-evident that language helps in teaching, that adults should help children, and that teachers should concentrate their work on material that is within the student's grasp? Indeed, doesn't this 'social constructivism' sound similar to the ideas which had been handed down from Plato, through Locke, Rousseau, and Froebel—ideas in the progressive tradition which stressed the importance of adults gently nurturing the cognitive growth of children?

The answer to those questions is yes. The message of Vygotsky and Bruner chimes in perfect harmony with that of the earlier progressive educators. The significance of their insights is in the antidote they provided to the almost fatalistic view of children's development which could be induced by Piaget's theory. While Piaget's theory could encourage a view of the child's intellectual development as an unwinding scroll of writing, that of Vygotsky and Bruner promoted a view of the writing being written as the child grew—it was variable and modifiable.

In Bruner's work, we see a more direct application of ideas to practice. He discusses teaching content with teaching method, such that something approaching an integrated theory of education seems to be appearing. With Bruner we see an appreciation of the 'guts' of a subject conjoined with a sensitivity about the way children learn. Bruner's first lesson was that there are *no* no-go areas when it comes to teaching and learning: anyone can learn almost anything if it is pitched at the right level and presented in the right way. (This contrasted, of course, with Piagetian ideas about 'readiness'.)

The teacher's job is thus not to ration out information, having decided what facts or skills need to be learned, but to encourage students to think in such a way that they understand a subject. Describing his own work, Bruner says: 'It seemed natural that emphasis should shift to teaching basic principles, underlying axioms, pervasive themes, that one should "talk physics" with students rather than "talk about" it to them.' The job is not just to transmit knowledge, it is to support the cultivation of intellectual skill.

The constructivist psychologists were important, too, because of the counterweight that they provided to another quite recent stream of thought—the third of the three theories about which I have spoken. This last, from the behaviourists, implied that learning, even learning of quite complex ideas, was best thought of as dissectible into discrete chunks which could be taught separately to the student in an environment which systematically rewarded success.

Behaviourism had been dismissed rather peremptorily by Plowden. It was, however, taken by some to offer the way forward to the sunlit uplands of problem-free learning. In particular, Harvard psychologist B.F. Skinner's operant conditioning—a view of learning that said everything, even the learning of language, came down to simple stimulus–response connections—was seen by many psychologists as the solution to all of education's problems. All we needed to do, said the behaviourists, was systematically analyse what needed to be learned, take a scalpel to a subject, and cut it into little bits—unequivocally learnable portions—then feed these to the learner in the most logical possible sequence. That's all there was to solving the problems of education: job done.

Though now discredited as a way of looking at complex learning, this simplistic idea was taken at the time to be the way forward by far too many people (including me, I'm ashamed to say, in the naivety of my youth). It led not just to the introduction of the silly but fairly harmless 'teaching machines' of the 1960s and 1970s, but far more seriously to the idea that you could tidily dissect the curriculum into bite-sized portions. During those decades this led in some schools, particularly special schools for children with learning difficulties, to the development of 'programmed instruction' and 'behavioural objectives' for learning and behaviour.

The consequence was the desertification of the curriculum as complex ideas were broken down into thousands of facts to be learned as behavioural objectives. You can imagine the view of teaching that would emerge if you subscribed to such a view. With a question such as 'What were the causes of the First World War?' your behavioural teacher-brain would be encouraged to follow the path of analysis-by-dissection-to-the-simplest-units: lists of dates, catalogues of countries and people, all lined up ready to be learned. Argument, thought, and discussion about interestingly divergent hypotheses would be sacrificed in favour of such easily learned units of information.

But people did, I'm glad to say, see the light, and the behavioural experiment turned out to be less of a branch in the tree of educational ideas and more of a short stump, mercifully chainsawed off when people realized it was growing out at a silly angle. (Rogue behavioural genes have, however, unfortunately remained in education's gene pool, ready to be requisitioned now by those who favour a structured curriculum with an emphasis on 'standards', accountability, and testing.)

The reason that so many of today's educators are inspired by the work of Vygotsky and Bruner is that both of these theorists bring clarity to the education narrative. Piaget and Skinner, by contrast, seemed sometimes to counter age-old truths about learning; the divergent directions which they set off about children's learning have often occluded or even contradicted the message of the progressive educators. The contribution of Vygotsky and Bruner is to have gathered the threads of the progressive thinking together again.

Testing, testing

Another offshoot of psychology proved to have a profound influence on the ways that education would develop: psychometrics, or the measurement of human abilities. Psychologists were excited about its potential at the beginning of the 20th century. Things had all started at Alfred Binet's Laboratory of Physiological Psychology at the Sorbonne, where the young French psychologist had developed tests of intelligence. Interest had quickly spread across the Atlantic and in 1916 the American psychologist Lewis Terman, developing Binet's work, coined the term 'intelligence quotient', or IQ. Terman asserted that 'The first task of the school would be to establish the native quality of every pupil; second, to supply the kind of instruction suited to each grade of ability' (p 336).

All of this was connected with presumptions about what intelligence was and how its measurement could help teachers.

Many early psychologists were making the assumption that intelligence was a characteristic endowed at birth in much the same way as height or hair colour. The corollary to this assumption was, of course, that there wasn't much that could be done about it: people had to make do with what they inherited. With fixity in intelligence, with little chance of improving people's native intelligence, it made sense to educate each according to their supposed potential. Psychometrics gave the promise of efficiently calibrating levels of ability, sorting the population for the most and least intelligent, and then educating differently children of differing levels of ability.

One psychologist in particular led the charge in arguing for this. This was Cyril Burt, who was appointed as the first ever psychologist for London in 1913. Burt was fascinated by the young technology of psychometrics. His quickly growing reputation, built on a phenomenal energy and a well written set of publications, his fondness for psychometrics, and his commitment to the idea that intelligence was inherited and more-or-less immutable all combined to give great stimulus to an increasingly segregative education system based on the categorization of the child via tests.

Although the interpretation of the facts is contested by some, there is very strong support for the thesis that Burt constructed data about the heritability of intelligence from non-existent studies of identical twins. Burt seems to have invented not only data, but also material and people to support his hereditarian hypothesis. As L.S. Hearnshaw, his biographer, explained: 'Of the more than forty "persons" who contributed reviews, notes and letters to [Burt's] journal during the period of Burt's editorship, well over half are unidentifiable, and judging from the style and content of their contributions were pseudonyms for Burt.' Almost more interesting than Burt's personal psychology in this chapter of deceit is his conviction in the legitimacy of the cause for which he was contriving evidence. Here was a man who had the highest respect for science, yet was prepared, it seems, to put his conviction in a deeper truth—that of the genetic basis for intelligence—above its systems and procedures.

Burt's fraud was discovered only after his death, but in happier times he had been one of the most influential contributors to the Hadow Committee and to the climate which gave rise to the 1944 Education Act in the UK, insofar as it related to the differentiation of children according to their ability. The members of the Hadow Committee, so forward-looking in many ways, had been persuaded by the highly plausible and convincing Burt that 'children need to be grouped according to their capacity, not merely in separate classes or standards, but in separate types of schools'.

The 1944 Act, alongside free secondary education for all, constructed a highly segregative post-war education system in Britain, dividing, supposedly, the clever from the not-so-clever, with the introduction of a set of tests at the age of eleven—the '11-plus'. These tests, in arithmetic, English, verbal and non-verbal reasoning, would do the job of dividing children into three types of school—grammar, secondary modern, and technical—for three types of mind: academic, practical, and technical. This segregated system had its rationale in Burt's specious psychological research.

The arguments had not been going all one way, though. The political scientist Walter Lippmann had in the early 1920s published a series of articles in the USA in which he argued that intelligence testers cleaved to a dogma about the heritability of intelligence, and that 'Intelligence testing in the hands of men who hold this dogma could not but lead to an intellectual caste system.' The perspicacity and prescience of Lippmann were borne out by later events: in the selective and segregative systems enabled and fostered by psychometrics were to be found precisely the caste system he predicted.

The findings of more sophisticated research eventually began to eat into the confidence of the hereditarians' position, particularly

"Doctor, I believe you've found the formula for success."

8. The work of many mid-century psychologists focused on the relative contributions of heredity and environment to school success

insofar as the views of the latter related to race as well as ability pure and simple. As Fienberg and Resnick put it, 'in the course of the 1920s, true believers became skeptics, and it appeared that the mainstream of American psychology had made a major paradigm shift, from race to culture, and from nature to nurture' (p 11). This change, they note, was due to the accumulating weight of evidence available in the psychological literature. Evidence came from many and varied sources: from exposure of the inappropriate statistical treatment of environmental influences in studies on racial difference; from studies which showed that blacks raised in the north of the USA had higher scores than whites from the south; from studies of southern-born black children raised in

New York which showed that the longer they had lived in New York, the higher their scores.

Despite all this, and notwithstanding the discovery of Burt's fraud, the momentum gathered by the intelligence-is-inherited position has enabled arguments about separate school systems to be put again and again through the recent history of schooling. In the 1960s the prominent educational psychologist Arthur Jensen was able to ask, in an influential paper in the *Harvard Educational Review*: 'Is there a danger that current welfare policies, unaided by eugenic foresight, could lead to the genetic enslavement of a substantial segment of our population?' The arguments continue to be made, as they have been more recently in *The Bell Curve* by Herrnstein and Murray.

Although there is a regular bubbling up of hereditarian views such as these, no one now, in the 21st century, could claim that hereditarian views are in the ascendant. Argument about the provenance of human ability now recognizes the complexity at play. However, the movement these views started has its legacy in the confidence people still feel to talk about ability as if this were a quality distributed at birth to be assessed and nurtured by schools in proportion to a student's 'potential'.

But the lesson of a century of research and reflection is that potential is multifaceted, ubiquitous, and crudely assessed through psychometrics. Sadly, the imprimatur of scientific respectability expropriated by psychometrics has been lent to programmes of testing that have not only distorted the curriculum, but destined generations of children to a second-rate schooling.

Breaking down the walls

Psychologists exerted their influence on education through their ideas about the ways children learn. Theirs is a child-centred view of education. Others have looked, by contrast, from the outside at the institution of the school and how it affects children's place in society. Sociologists have looked at gender, race, class, and disability to examine how and why school maintains or even exaggerates differences between children, how it creates stigma, or how it incorrectly identifies as 'problems' children from certain backgrounds.

Let's take selection as a brief introductory example, since I focused just now on its growth following the advice of psychologists such as Burt. Analysis revealed that far from providing the gateway to a better future for 'bright' working-class youngsters that its champions proclaimed it would, the existence of the selective system was in fact merely reproducing or even widening differences of opportunity for the young populace. As the Crowther Report, *15 to 18*, put it memorably in 1959, for most working-class children 'Jude was still likely to remain obscure' unless they went to grammar school; but only a very small proportion of them did. That report drew on a wide range of research, which all pointed in the same direction: the selective system wasted talent and, furthermore, it wasn't producing the skills and adaptability in young people that were needed in a rapidly changing society.

Talk to the hand

The contemporary saying among young people, 'Talk to the hand' (meaning 'I'm not going to listen'), sums up the attitude of very large numbers of children at school. A substantial minority of schools' inhabitants hear little of what is said to them at school and care less. This is borne out both by casual observation and by official statistics: in the UK around 40 per cent of school leavers finish their ten years of compulsory education without even what is taken to be the most basic measure of a satisfactory education (namely GCSE examination passes in English and mathematics at grades A* to C). The statistic is as consistent as it is depressing.

And things haven't improved much over the years despite a
bewildering array of new initiatives from governments to improve
what they call 'the performance' of schools.

Why are schools so unsuccessful with such large numbers of
young people? You would think that the time and money invested
in teaching some quite simple kinds of knowledge at school
would have more effect. As President George W. Bush put the
problem so memorably in 2004, 'Then you wake up at the high
school level and find out that the illiteracy level of our children
are appalling.' Quite. Politicians are always trying to address this
thorny question and their answers have generally settled, as we
have seen, on poor teaching or teaching the wrong things in the
wrong way. Education professionals—teachers, headteachers,
teacher trainers—are taken to be more concerned with high-
minded ideals about social justice than with the basic needs of
the children and young people in their charge. In 1993, UK prime
minister John Major summed up the sentiment in urging
everyone to get 'back to basics'.

Many agree with this sentiment, though there are alternative
explanations for the failure of so many children at school. One
such concerns the different cultures of school and home: many
children don't do well at school simply because they don't
understand what is going on there. We've known for decades that
this is the case: you learn about the environment in which you
live, and if this is very different from that of the school, you won't
learn much at school.

You don't find many children from travellers' families succeeding
even in the very basics at school, let alone going to Oxford or
Harvard. A revealing statistic from an education charity, the
Sutton Trust, makes the point well: in three years, the universities
at Oxford and Cambridge accepted 946 pupils from just five 'top'
schools in the UK (four of them private), while they admitted
fewer, only 927, from another 2,000 schools and colleges.

We're looking at achievement measured by the pinnacle of academic success here, but the capillaries of this problem run right through education, not just in the admissions to top universities. Those from certain kinds of background emerge from school not just a little worse off but much worse off than those from more advantaged backgrounds. What causes such disparities? Surely it cannot simply be the quality of education on offer at different schools. One general answer to this question was proposed by the sociologist Basil Bernstein, who came up with an interesting insight on the consequences of differences between the cultures of school and home and in particular the kinds of language used in those different places.

He suggested that a child's social class often imposes different kinds of language use on its members. There are two basic kinds of language, or 'codes' as Bernstein called them, which allow us to navigate our ways through life. There is an elaborated or 'posh' register used by the world of officialdom, and, importantly, by school; and there is a restricted code used by friends and family for most of the encounters of everyday life. The restricted code is used where there is a kind of implicit understanding between speakers: it's short and sweet, pointing hearers to a mass of shared but unspoken meaning.

For the elaborated code, though, everything is distinctly spelt out. It uses longer sentences, is more complex in its structure, and employs more unusual words. At school, most of the intercourse happens using the formalities of the elaborated code. Not only are lessons conducted using the elaborated code but also the instructions about what to do, how to conduct yourself, where to go.

The problem for working-class children, said Bernstein, is that they have little experience with the elaborated code, so when they get to school they are instantly alienated from much that goes on there. They don't understand, literally, what teachers are talking about. Middle-class children, by contrast, are familiar with both codes and are able to switch between the one and the other. What do working-class children do in this situation? They may pick up the elaborated code and if they do all is fine and dandy: they benefit from the acquisition. Often, though, they simply withdraw, opt out, or rebel. However assertive the retreat from school becomes, its inevitable consequences are in the markedly poorer achievements of these children at school—the 40 per cent who don't even reach basic levels of competence.

Disadvantage comes also from inequality, either within a society or within a school. The difference between the most and least favoured has effects on both achievement and behaviour. (Epidemiologists call these effects 'gradient effects'.) Students do worse in a broad range of outcomes—from behavioural adjustment, to literacy, to mathematics achievement—when there are larger inequalities between students in a school. The epidemiologist Sir Michael Marmot puts it this way: 'Inequalities in educational outcomes are as persistent as those for health and are subject to a similar social gradient. Despite many decades of policies aimed at equalising educational opportunities, the attainment gap remains.' Doug Willms, a Canadian epidemiologist, has shown that exaggerating difference between students in different schools or within the same school can have serious consequences. He notes, for example, that when students are segregated, either between classes or tracks within schools, students from disadvantaged backgrounds do worse.

For a long time the response of educators to issues of differential success was framed in terms of 'compensatory' or 'therapeutic' education. It was assumed that something was lacking in the culture of the child, or that there was something wrong in a child's emotional make-up which needed to be put right. The response was implicitly to load the fault on to the children, their culture, or psychological make-up. Rather than questioning the institution of the school or the nature of the curriculum, policymakers and principals preferred to see children who didn't fit as 'disturbed' or 'special'. What this attitude did, though, was to divert attention from the fact that school offers an environment which is almost as alien to some young people as another planet. The solution perhaps is to look again at the nature of school and I examine in Chapter 7 the ideas of some of those who have done this.

Chapter 6
The curriculum

In 1939 a satire was published about the curriculum. By the American educator Harold Benjamin (but written under the pseudonym J. Abner Peddiwell) and entitled *The Saber-tooth Curriculum*, it has become a classic. It tells a series of tales about an imaginary Neolithic tribe which develops a curriculum for its schoolchildren based on fish-grabbing, horse-clubbing, and sabre-tooth tiger-scaring. All was going well for the tribe until an ice age transformed the environment: the fish became scarcer and fleeter; horses and tigers disappeared completely. So, new skills more relevant to the new environment were cultivated by tribe members: net-making, antelope-scaring, and bear-pit-digging. But while these new skills had been developed, those in charge of the schools rejected the suggestion that the school curriculum should be reworked to teach them: 'That wouldn't be education,' they said. The traditionalists insisted that the new skills would just be 'training'.

Those arguing for change were furious: 'But damn it…how can any person with good sense be interested in such useless activities? What is the point in teaching to catch fish with the bare hands when it can't be done any more?' The traditionalists replied with a refrain familiar in debates about the curriculum: 'Don't be foolish,' they said. 'We don't teach fish-grabbing to grab fish; we teach it to develop a generalized agility which can never be developed by

"To learn tiger-scaring, it is quite helpful to have a real tiger."

9. With *The Saber-tooth Curriculum*, Harold Benjamin made the point that much of the curriculum is inappropriate for students' needs

mere training.' They silenced the radicals with the argument that true education is timeless, enduring through changing conditions like solid rock. There were, they said, 'eternal verities, and the saber-tooth curriculum is one of them!'

The debate is as old as the hills. Indeed, as I write, a new 'Free School' is opening in London—one of a clutch of such schools across England—and as I watch the TV news there are pictures of its children learning Latin. The school's founders and the parents all seem to think this is an excellent idea. The arguments that are being evinced for the learning of Latin are much the same as those promoted by the sabre-tooth curriculum traditionalists: eternal verities, training the mind, agility in thinking, rules of language, etc., etc.

The great mathematician and philosopher A.N. Whitehead took a keen interest in education. When he saw this kind of thing happening he lamented that education in moribund skills and activities was not only useless—it was harmful. In *The Aims of*

Education and other essays he said: 'In the history of education, the most striking phenomenon is that schools of learning, which at one epoch are alive with a ferment of genius, in a succeeding generation exhibit merely pedantry and routine.'

If you think that learning complicated stuff like Latin conjugations is useful because it provides good training in thinking, then allow me to offer some evidence that contests this popular myth. For, as with many beliefs about learning and education, there is a treasure chest of evidence that remains mainly unopened by those who voice opinions on these subjects. If you do open it you find that psychologists—one hundred years ago more than now (given that the issue is now taken to be more or less settled)—have been interested in what they have inelegantly called 'transfer of training'. You find that ever since William James, the Victorian psychologist (and brother of novelist Henry), failed to boost his 'memory muscle' by doing memory exercises there has been a consistent failure to find evidence for the proposition that learning skill X will boost your ability in skill Y. There is no evidence that this is the case, but for some reason we carry on believing that doing complicated puzzles of one kind or another—or, indeed, learning a dead language—trains us in thinking. It's one of those widely believed fallacies that seems to be impervious to the intrusion of evidence which might contradict it.

A fine example of the non-transfer of skill exists in chess playing. It's one of the most studied skills by psychologists, because its need for sequencing ideas, using memory, developing projection, and imagination ought to fire up the neurons like nothing else: chess players should be top-notch problem solvers, with all the practice they get. But sadly they're not; they're the same as the rest of us. What top chess players are good at is playing chess. And the fact that they don't do much other than play chess means that there's not much else they're good at. The moral? You get good at what you practise, not at what you don't.

As I anticipate arguments likely to be posed by the proponents of the teaching of dead languages I'm reminded of a quotation from the French philosopher Simone Weil in *The Need for Roots*: 'Culture is an instrument wielded by professors to manufacture professors, who when their turn comes, will manufacture professors.' In other words, what we choose to talk about as educators—or even just as educated people—is that which reflects our own backgrounds, interests, and predilections. It's just as true of teachers in schools as it is of professors in universities: the curriculum is shaped by adults thinking that young people need what they themselves were fed as young people. Thus is the curriculum reproduced.

Thinking about the curriculum is not just about the consideration of matters such as the relevance of teaching dead languages. For what we want children to learn leads us also to the way we choose to teach, and this goes back to the formal–progressive debate of Chapter 2. Should our teaching focus on instruction in basic skills or should we be trying to inspire and enthuse children, stirring their imaginations?

The secret garden

Where do ideas about what we should teach come from? The received wisdom among politicians is that the origins of the curriculum have always been a bit of a mystery, concocted in dark rooms by cabals of teachers, many of them clearly of a Trotskyite persuasion. In fact, one UK minister of education, David Eccles, in 1960 famously called the curriculum a 'secret garden' and this has become something of a cliché, to be repeated by UK prime minister James Callaghan when he began his 'Great Debate' on education in his Ruskin College speech in 1979. Among the political class, the generally accepted feeling seems to have been that the curriculum has been the jealously guarded province of teachers and educational professionals, never to be penetrated by the common sense of politicians or public. It was this feeling that led to the establishment of the National Curriculum in the UK and a clutch of other European countries in the 1980s.

That National Curriculum for England now comprises twelve subjects which are, at the time of writing, statutory at the secondary stage: art and design, citizenship, design and technology, English, geography, history, ICT (information and communications technology), mathematics, modern foreign languages, music, physical education, and science. Most of these, barring citizenship and modern foreign languages, are compulsory also at the primary stage.

Recent moves in the USA have aimed to introduce similar conformity. In 2010 the Common Core State Standards Initiative sought to corral diverse state curricula into the same pen. The initiative aims to:

> provide a consistent, clear understanding of what students are expected to learn, so teachers and parents know what they need to do to help them. The standards are designed to be robust and relevant to the real world, reflecting the knowledge and skills that our young people need for success in college and careers.

Almost all of the USA's fifty states have joined the initiative. As part of it, at least 85 per cent of state curricula will be based on the Standards, which are accompanied by a testing regime, notionally to measure student achievement, but in practice, of course—and equally importantly—measuring teacher and school achievement.

All this activity by governments to manage the curriculum has been in response to the 'secret garden' assumptions about its construction and a mistrust of the dominant role of autonomous professionals in that process of construction. But if you look at that curriculum down the ages you find that there is very little evidence that educators have been secretly conspiring to devise and manipulate it for purposes of social engineering. The truth is more prosaic. The truth is that the curriculum has always existed more or less in its current form, as a product mainly of habit and tradition.

In fact, the modern-day lists of prescribed subjects are not too different from those contained in the 1904 Regulations for Secondary Schools in Great Britain, which gave an official declaration of what should be in the curriculum: arithmetic, algebra, drawing for boys and needlework for girls, English, French, geography, history, physical education, science, and singing.

And they are not too different—if rather more extended—from the list described by Aristotle in *Politics*: 'Roughly four things are generally taught to children: reading and writing, physical training, music, and, not always included, drawing.' One wonders what it is about this inventory of subjects, replicated in education systems across the world, which is so resistant to change. Is it likely that educators have distilled the essence of good education in these ten subjects (give or take two or three)?

The constant curriculum

It's salutary to look more broadly at curricula far and wide and down the ages to enable some lateral thinking on the issue. If you do this, you'll see that ancient curricula comprised a mix of familiar and not-so-familiar topics. Confucius, for example, said that students should study good manners. The ancient Greeks based their broader curriculum around 'harmonics', which were astronomy, arithmetic, geometry, and music. The Romans, as we have seen, were uncommonly fond of rhetoric. Each of those had its influence on the medieval curriculum of the *trivium*—of grammar, logic, and rhetoric—and the *quadrivium*, of arithmetic, astronomy, geometry, and music. In our own schools until relatively recently the learning of Latin occupied a high proportion of the curriculum: in the year of Shakespeare's birth,

1564, Sir Humphrey Gilbert responded to a general sense of unease about the emphasis on Latin in schools (for parents were complaining that their children were forgetting how to use their native tongue) with a plan for a new kind of practical school, or academy, that would focus on the use of English and other modern languages, and also civil policy, mathematics, astronomy, navigation, and medicine.

A respectable case could be made for some of the less familiar of these ideas to become incorporated into our own curriculum today. The 'rhetoric' beloved of the Romans, concerned as it is with the use of the spoken word, would seem to be a prime candidate for rediscovery in a world so dependent on the use of spoken language. Confucius's 'manners', if my recent journey on top of a Birmingham bus is anything to go by, wouldn't go amiss.

The astute American commentator on education Neil Postman argued compellingly for a curriculum built around what he called 'the three As' (as distinct from the three Rs): astronomy, archaeology, and anthropology. Astronomy, favourite of the Greeks, would cultivate in the young a sense of awe, interdependence, and global responsibility. Archaeology and anthropology should be taught because an understanding of the timelessness not only of ideas but of the trials and tribulations of people—of their grief and happiness—tells us of our connection with other people. We shall find those connections in the writing and art of others long before us, whether Sumerian, Babylonian, Egyptian, or Chinese. All of them 'complained, grieved, rejoiced ... scolded their children, fell in battle' just as people in Kansas City do today.

An equally plausible case is made for an alternative curriculum by Guy Claxton in *What's the Point of School?* Eschewing a subject-based curriculum, he suggests that today's curriculum would more profitably be based around qualities and habits of mind rather than subjects. He argues that it should centre around topics such as statistics and probability and managing risk, human rights, ecology, global awareness, ethics, body awareness, and around 'qualities' such as empathy, the ability to negotiate, collaboration, scepticism, willpower, and relaxation. The shifts in emphasis that would accompany such a change would, perhaps, make the potential meaning and usefulness of school more conspicuous to its inhabitants.

Following the 20th-century philosopher Michael Oakeshott, though, we might conclude that arguments for any such instrumentally based curricula are misplaced. For Oakeshott, the subjects of the curriculum—history, mathematics, science, and so on—offer ways of capturing and understanding the world; they are a precious legacy passed to new generations, says Oakeshott, bequeathing treasuries of stories, models of understanding, and frames of analysis. Using these, learners find ways of comprehending and imagining. The job of the teacher, he suggested, is to induct new generations of learners into established forms of understanding: there is no purpose in a curriculum separate from this.

Spirals and cubes

The curriculum isn't just about content. The great educator Lawrence Stenhouse suggested that the curriculum should be thought of as a set of interrelating cogs: there are activities to be carried out by the teacher; there is subject matter; there are generalized patterns of behaviour; and there is understanding. The main point he was making was that the curriculum is not, in practical terms, simply about knowledge to be transmitted, but about how that knowledge is handled—or even how it is transcended—by teachers to enable understanding in their charges. The subject matter itself, the knowledge, while important, is less important than the opportunities it offers for the development of thinking. Knowledge, Stenhouse suggested, should principally be seen in the curriculum as a medium for thinking.

His point is perhaps doubly true today, when knowledge pure and simple—facts, information—is so easily located. It's no wonder that down the ages, in fact until the dawn of the Internet, knowledge was treated as if it were hidden treasure: what can now be found in seconds may have taken days or weeks to find, so the more that could be stored in the head, the better equipped a person was for life. The world of knowledge has been turned on its head in a period of only two decades or so by the Internet, and in our thinking about the curriculum we haven't yet worked through the consequences.

Stenhouse offered another analogy about the curriculum, beyond meshing cogs. He said that the curriculum could be thought of as a game, complete with its players and its hardware—its pieces, board, and so on. These parts, the hardware, are similar to the 'subjects' of a curriculum—the content, the raw materials. While the hardware provides the materials for the game, the *kind* of game that follows—good or bad, quick or slow, thoughtful or perfunctory—depends on the moves made by the players. The

10. The world of knowledge has been turned on its head. Have we thought through the consequences?

hardware is relatively unimportant. The same is true for the curriculum: the kind of teaching that happens depends not just on the subject matter but on the ways in which it is interpreted—the skill with which it is transformed—for the benefit of the students. The key is in the skill of the teacher.

In making this point, he had an eye to the extent to which the *content* of the curriculum could hypnotize its developers and users. Not only could there be too much emphasis on the nuts and bolts of the curriculum, with too little attention to what was done with those bits and pieces, but those mechanical parts could lead their users, the teachers, to become mechanics rather than mentors. With such an outlook they would inevitably be putting the stress on the parts—their sequencing, construction, acquisition, and so on—rather than on understanding. Assessment of what was going on following the teaching could thus become mechanized, stressing the learning of facts and the coverage of material, with scant attention to the real grasp that students had made of that material. Had they understood? Had they gained insights? Did they develop new awareness?

In this sense, the idea that an outside body—a government or a set of advisers—can 'teacher-proof' a body of knowledge in a prescribed curriculum is 'nonsense', asserts Jerome Bruner, since without reflexivity in the relationship, without the to-ing and fro-ing between teacher and student, little understanding is likely to happen; little *education* happens. The obverse is also true: Bruner tells the story of a teacher colleague who noted that when you teach well, it seems as if three-quarters of the students are above average. All practising teachers will concur.

None of this is to say that content is irrelevant or meaningless. Rather, it is to say that content becomes a too-easy focus and a lot more thought needs to be given to the 'how' as well as the 'what' of a curriculum. Bruner discusses the need for teachers to:

- appreciate students' need to learn the structure of a subject, rather than just mastery of facts and techniques. This is the hardest of all tasks for the teacher, relating this fact to that and earlier points to later points. Only in this way do the lineaments of the subject become clear—only in this way does a mental map of a subject emerge for a student.

- reassess the significance of 'readiness' for the student. For many years educators became almost obsessed with doing things in the right order, and not tackling subjects that children weren't, supposedly, at the right 'cognitive stage' to understand. Some teacher educators had become fixated with the ideas of Jean Piaget, who, as we have seen, had suggested that children passed through fixed stages which marked their capacity and readiness for thinking. They couldn't skip a stage, or they would be unable to cope with the task set at the higher cognitive level. Drawing on other psychological models, Bruner said this was mistaken. He made the controversial assertion that children could, in some shape or form, grasp almost any idea. They are always 'ready' for learning and it is the job of the teacher not slavishly to follow some formula about cognitive development but rather to use their experience and empathy to teach material as the time seems right. It is in this context that he discussed the *spiral curriculum*: 'One starts somewhere—where the learner *is*,' says Bruner (p ix). Then the teacher should revisit these basic ideas repeatedly, building on them.

- recognize that alongside instrumental and scientific forms of thinking there is also structure given to thought and its development by *narrative*. The ready-made meaning structures in narrative should be grasped and employed enthusiastically by the teacher. Children should be taught how to think by using the shrewd guess, the fertile hypothesis, the courageous leap. The teaching of such thinking skills should be at the centre of the curriculum.

- understand that children should want to study for study's own sake, for learning's sake, not for the sake of good grades or examination success. The curriculum should, in other words, be interesting. (Yes, it sounds too obvious even to say, but sometimes the emphasis on content has trumped all other considerations, including that of making learning interesting.)

Ted Wragg, a highly respected education researcher, added to the debate with his notion of a 'cubic curriculum'. The curriculum, he suggested, can be thought of as being three-dimensional, like a cube, with three planes. The first plane is that of the subjects: maths, English, science, geography, and so on. The second is formed of cross-curricular themes such as citizenship or language or imagination. And the third contains different teaching styles such as discovery, observation, teamwork, demonstration, or practice.

The important point about Wragg's cubic model and Bruner's spiral one before it is that there is no either/or about the way that the curriculum is conceived. It is not *either* subject knowledge *or* the development of imagination through project work. Rather, it is a question of integrating forms of information and styles of learning in such a way that the learner learns usefully and meaningfully, with understanding.

The hidden curriculum

Aside from the straightforwardly visible curriculum there is the hidden curriculum. This exists in the wider set of beliefs and values pupils acquire because of the way that a school is run and its teaching organized. It is about the behaviour of the teachers, the textbooks chosen, the school rules. Does the school, for example, through the way that authority is allocated to pupils— perhaps through a prefect system—tell pupils anything about the staff's opinion on the distribution and use of power in society more generally? How are those prefects chosen—by staff or students?—and what does the system that is used teach pupils about democracy? If all the senior staff in the school are male does this tell the children something about gender and power? What kind of textbooks are used—do they encourage children to think, or do they spoon-feed facts and figures? Do they give a particular slant on contested matters?

Marshall's history textbook *Our Island Story*, popular in British schools until quite recently, exemplifies the last point well. In it, the history of Britain is given as beginning with savagery, rising over two millennia ultimately toward civilization and harmony. With the story told largely via the reigns of monarchs and the gallant deeds of brave knights, readers are given a particular view of Britain's story. There's little sign of social history: never mind how the peasants lived, toiled, and died. One of the book's final chapters is entitled 'Victoria—from Cannibal to Christian', the message being that with Victoria, Britain had reached the pinnacle of civilization—the Christian nation. As the author puts it:

> From the very beginning of our story you have seen how Britons have fought for freedom, and how step by step they have won it, until at last Britons live under just laws and have themselves the power to make these laws.

One has to note that in constructing the idea of 'cannibal to Christian', the *Island Story* omits to mention some of the important yet ignoble chapters toward the end of the story, when Christian civilization's apogee should surely have been attained. There is no mention, for example, of the opium wars (1839–60) in which Her Majesty's ships pounded the coast of China after the emperor of that country had had the temerity to outlaw opium. The only consideration in Her Majesty's government's action at that time seemed to have been to protect the East India Company's handsome profits from the opium trade.

The choice of this as a textbook for the teaching of history would present some clear messages about values, civilization, race, class relations, and much more. We have, though, to note that the use of such a book is applauded, not questioned, by some contemporary commentators: the education editor of the *Daily Telegraph* suggested that '*Our Island Story* is a marvellous antidote to the fractured, incoherent history most primary school children are taught today' (16 June 2005). The *Telegraph*'s education editor is not alone in such a sentiment about the content of school history books: in 1934 Joseph Stalin had regaled a meeting of historians, as David Cannadine and his colleagues recount in *The Right Kind of History*, with these words: 'These textbooks aren't good for anything. History must be history.' Cannadine notes that what Stalin meant was that history should be a 'triumphant cavalcade of national heroes'.

Philip Jackson, in his 1968 classic, *Life in Classrooms*, asserts that the hidden curriculum goes even deeper than this kind of embedded message. It lies in 'the crowds, the praise, and the power' (p 33) of the classroom, and learning to live in a classroom is learning to live in a crowd, with all that this entails. Teachers, in order to control the crowd, employ rewards and sanctions which relate both to the hidden curriculum—how the student deals with the crowds, the turmoil, the petty unfairnesses—and its obverse, the official curriculum, or the academic demands of school.

Jackson makes the point that the rewards which are offered in both the hidden and the official curriculum are for the convenience of the school and its smooth running: children are rewarded for compliance, for docility, for conformity in thinking rather than ingenuity. Are these really the characteristics that we want to promote in our young people, asks Jackson. (Maybe they actually are: as Everett Reimer points out in his classic anti-school treatise *School Is Dead*, the Ottomans used to castrate their candidates for top civil service posts to make them more biddable and docile; Reimer suggests that 'Schools make the physical emasculation unnecessary by doing the job more effectively at the libidinal level' (p 18).)

Testing can drive the curriculum

Returning to Stenhouse for a moment, the problem with looking at the curriculum as knowledge to be transmitted, he said, is that it imposes a double whammy of distortion to education. For, in a culture of performativity, the solid material of the curriculum, the content, lends itself admirably to being tested as governments seek to make teachers more accountable. It's as if notions of accountability and testing are in symbiosis. A vicious circle can then be entered as content—that is to say, collections of facts—is chopped up and delivered in neat boxes ready for assessment. The curriculum, seen as solid material to be 'delivered', lends itself to the accountability-testing symbiosis in the way that understanding does not.

You can't slice up and measure students' understanding nearly as easily as you can measure those same students' retention of facts: it is much easier to set and mark a multiple-choice question about, say, the causes of global warming, than it is to set and mark an essay on the same subject. The latter assesses students' ability to argue, analyse, and mix ideas while the former tests only the retention of bald facts. The problem here is that this ease of measurement itself actually shapes teaching. The cart, in the shape of assessment, is put before the horse, in the shape of understanding.

The damaging consequences of this are amplified by the enormous stress that politicians put on the results of assessment. If funding for your school depends on the results of assessment, or if your continued employment as a teacher depends on some set of tests, then you have to be a pretty strong-willed teacher to avoid the temptation to 'teach to the test', rather than engaging in a form of education that will not so readily meet the outcomes, usually measured against 'standards' of one kind or another, demanded by the testing regime. Thus, a series of facts to be learned becomes a more attractive proposition than an animated discussion, perhaps with no clear resolution, with the youngsters you teach. Under such a regime, some of the essentials of the educated mind—respect for uncertainty, acknowledgement of different opinions, recognition of the tentativeness of knowledge— become buried.

One of the most significant consequences of the proliferation of tests over the last decades of the 20th century and the first of the 21st has been this tendency of assessment to direct the curriculum. Like a huge magnet, assessment drags the curriculum toward it. It should, of course, even if we accept a need for tests, be the other way round: the curriculum should be independent of any consideration of tests: tests should be constructed and administered in another space, both literally and metaphorically, hermetically sealed not only from the teacher's gaze but also—and even more importantly—from the teacher's consideration.

In practice, though, this never happens. It is inevitable that if you decide regularly to test children's performance on the curriculum, and if, furthermore, you make teachers' careers and schools' futures depend on the results, the tests will very quickly come to dominate what is taught. Not only the content but also the style and manner of the teaching will be influenced by the tests. Teaching will be about getting the right answer, irrespective of understanding: it will become monotonous, stereotyped. And the prevalence and power of testing seem to coarsen the process of education. There is much evidence, for example, that cheating—or just 'helping'—occurs: in parts of the USA, legal action has been taken against teachers who have helped students in the important tests that would take them from one stage of schooling to the next (sometimes called 'high-stakes' tests). In some parts of the world there is flagrant corruption: invigilators are bribed, candidates impersonated by more able friends, and examination papers sold in advance.

And there is little evidence that any of this is changing. In fact, in many parts of the world it is getting worse. In the 1990s the cram schools that coached Japanese young people in high-stakes tests were limited to Japan, but they have spread to other parts of Asia and to the USA. In Japan, 40 per cent of students or more attend these cram schools, or *juku*, with young people giving up much of their leisure time to attend for two or three hours each evening and on Saturdays. In China, parents—in their desperation to help their children do better in the crucial college entrance examinations, the *gaokao*—have become prey to barmy snake-oil programmes that promise to boost 'right-brain' thinking.

One hopes that there will come greater recognition of the damage done to the fabric of the curriculum—to the quality of education—by the accountability-testing mindset.

Chapter 7
School's out!

From century to century the edifice of the school, both in its actual building and in its practices and routines, has held firm. The law continues to oblige parents to send their offspring to an institution organized broadly on military lines where children will be instructed in the subjects taken to be important for the smooth running of society. Teachers continue to stand in front of classes and teach lessons where, as we have seen, the menu of subjects on offer has remained broadly constant. Across the world, from Africa to Asia, the pattern is copied.

Where does this formula for schooling get us? At the beginning of this book I noted some comments from Mark Twain, Winston Churchill, and Albert Einstein which dismissed as irrelevant or even harmful the experience provided by school. Those three people are pretty impressive as envoys of any message and we should listen carefully to their counsel.

Most school students are surely not far away from them in their attitude. Most will agree that the '*Back to school!*' notice that appears in supermarkets in August is the most depressing sight of late summer, if not the whole year. And while I know of no popular songs celebrating the joys of school, there are plenty whose lyrics point to its miseries for the student. Alice Cooper's 'No more teachers/No more books/No more teachers' dirty looks'

11. Across the world, the pattern of teachers in classrooms is copied

is similar in its sentiment to Pink Floyd's 'We don't need no education/We don't need no thought control/No dark sarcasm in the classroom...'

There is a mismatch between the clichés of inclusiveness, achievement, and happiness promulgated by the education establishment and the gloom that school habitually invokes. For many children, just the smell of early September school—polish and paint—invokes symptoms of mild phobia: nausea, a sinking feeling, and a strong desire to run away. For many others school is all right (but little more than all right) and for a small number it is a refuge and a relief. Some like it, especially at the primary stage. But there can be no doubt that for a large minority of young people—around 40 per cent—it does little or nothing, providing a profoundly unenlightening experience which is recoiled from in a kind of desultory opposition.

Why the dislike? Not because teachers don't try hard. Teachers are surely the most dedicated professionals, encouraging, enthusing, and inspiring their charges, and, as 1970s prime minister Harold Wilson noted, for many children coming from his kind of background, they can be the most important adults in the world. Critics have suggested that the problem may be that school is simply an inappropriate place for most young people. It offers them nothing that they want or need and they come out with precious little.

Those critics, of various shapes and hues, have focused on different elements of the enterprise of school. There are first of all those who say that school doesn't pay: it doesn't provide the unalloyed benefits for both state and individual which are proclaimed by politicians. Then there are those who see school as a rights-free zone, quashing the originality and creativity of youth. Yet others condemn it as counterproductive even in the most traditional terms, failing to instil basic skills. I'll look at some of these criticisms in turn.

School doesn't pay

Across the world, money is pumped into education by governments in the belief that a better-schooled workforce will lead to improved economic growth. And it's a shibboleth of modern life that school means betterment for everyone. There is little challenge from taxpayers about the money spent on education because nearly all subscribe to these beliefs; they assume that for themselves, their children, or grandchildren, more education (that is to say, more certificates) will lead to better job prospects and higher earnings. These beliefs have led to a massive growth in schooling (in its widest sense, to include university) from the end of the 19th century, when school attendance was made compulsory; during the 20th century school leaving ages rose steadily, and the demand for, and supply of, certification mushroomed. This can be witnessed in the USA over the past century in the rise of the award of Bachelor's degrees:

- In 1900 barely 27,000 Bachelor's degrees were awarded.
- By 1950 half a million were awarded per year.
- The million-a-year mark was reached in 1988.
- By 2010, one and a half million degrees were awarded each year.

...which represents a fifty-five-fold increase in the award of degrees in the USA in just over a century.

Demand for education has never been stronger and institutions have gladly supplied the product to meet the demand. Despite the belief in education, though, there has been an accumulating body of evidence to show that in fact there is no simple equation relating benefits such as economic growth or individuals' life prospects to schooling. In reality, school seems to do little to transform people's opportunities. As early as 1966 James S. Coleman revealed that differences among schools mattered much less in the determination of outcomes than their students' family backgrounds. Christopher Jencks, a Harvard academic, came in for a lot of criticism a few years later for coming to much the same conclusion in his book *Inequality: A reassessment of the effect of family and schooling in America*.

The best analyses of recent years disclose much the same message about school, though such analyses are unpalatable to many and their authors have to endure some funny looks from politicians. As Alison Wolf puts it in her forensic analysis *Does Education Matter?*, 'Questioning the automatic value of any rise in the education budget, it seems, places one somewhere between an animal-hater and an imbecile.' The powerful argument she makes from the evidence she adduces, if I can try and summarize it in a few lines, is that the relationship of schooling to all sorts of beneficial outcomes is real, but any conclusion that the schooling actually *causes* the benefits is mistaken. As she puts it, the apparent returns from schooling 'reflect its use to sort people' and those people would get sorted one way or another anyway, with or without schools. Nor is there any clear link between economic growth and spending on education.

John Marsh draws mainly from American data in his powerful book *Class Dismissed* to emerge with conclusions broadly similar to Wolf's. He puts a different spin on his analysis, though, noting that the huge amounts nations spend on education do little to improve the life chances of those students who possess few of the advantages of life. He goes back to a quotation from Jencks's *Inequality* to sum up his point: 'the characteristics of a school's output depends largely on a single input, namely, the characteristics of the entering children.' Marsh concludes, like Jencks, that schools fail to equalize or even alter the distribution of opportunity for their students.

Wolf regrets the fact that developing countries are, expensively, copying the achievement-orientated, educationally barren models of the West. In a response to a critique of her analysis she concludes: 'I don't think anyone who knows developing countries doubts that education can be a sterile rat-race. Worse, the belief that education can deliver growth offers an easy way of avoiding our own obligations.'

We don't need no thought control

As we have seen, dissatisfaction with the traditions and routines of school has been a constant refrain through schooling's story. A theme through this has been concern about the persistent regimentation of the school, which often operated, critics such as philosopher Bertrand Russell said, as a cross between a prison and an army camp. Highly critical of the disciplined and restricted structure of state education, these critics set up their own schools. Most notably, A.S. Neill started Summerhill in the UK, and the Sudbury schools began in the USA, following Dewey's progressive Laboratory School in Chicago.

A.S. Neill's Summerhill School was set up in 1921 in Suffolk, England. Neill's vision was certainly in the progressive tradition but it extended that tradition to a consideration of the role played by adult authority in young people's development. Neill was influenced by the psychoanalytic theories of Sigmund Freud and Wilhelm Reich to believe that the imposition of authority led to fear and the inhibition of expression in the child. He envisaged a community in which children would be free from adult authority. As the school operates today, its students, or, rather, the members of the community, are free to do what they wish, as long they do not cause any harm to others. Their liberty extends to the freedom to choose which lessons, if any, they attend.

The emphasis on freedom led Summerhill into several skirmishes with authority in the shape of the national school inspectorate in England, most notably in an inspection which was used as a basis for an attempt to close down the school at the end of the 1990s. The school challenged the findings of the inspection and the attempts to close the school had eventually to be dropped by the Department for Education and Employment following some caustic comments from the judge about the quality of the Department's case.

In commenting on the case, the human rights lawyer Geoffrey Robertson places Neill's contribution high in the development of human rights law, arguing that Neill pioneered the idea that 'children have rights, that they are not owned by parents or teacher, that it is a crime to assault them physically and a serious mistake to force them to act against their will except out of consideration for others'. As he notes, these ideas were revolutionary—anarchic, even—back in the 1920s. They are now, however, taken to be uncontroversial and are to be found enshrined in the 1989 UN convention on the rights of the child.

Another reaction to the regimentation of school has been in the home-schooling movement, which isn't as new as you might imagine. In the late 18th century, 'domestic education' became fashionable among the more affluent middle classes and gentry, partly in response to John Locke and others having inveighed against the segregation of children at school. After Locke, Rousseau had counselled: 'Poverty, pressure of business, mistaken social prejudice, none of them can excuse a man from his duty, which is to support and educate his own children.' Charlotte Mason, a prominent English educator and home-education advocate in the later 19th century, while a devotee of Rousseau and his ideas, had painted his influence in this regard almost as Rasputin-like: 'Under the spell of his teaching, people in the fashionable world…retired from the world, sometimes even left their husbands, to work hard at the classics, mathematics, sciences, that they might with their own lips instruct their children.'

The fashion for domestic education for the wealthy lasted well into the 19th century, with, at one time, up to 30 per cent of the offspring of affluent families being educated at home. Today, the home education movement is driven by motives not dissimilar to those which impelled its 18th- and 19th-century advocates, but it is a far more multicoloured phenomenon now, the reasons for the rejection of state-funded education being many and varied. It's difficult to assess how many children are home educated, but estimates in Britain vary between one in 200 and one in a thousand. The recent intellectual stimulus for home education was greatly reinforced by the thinking of characters such as John Holt (whom we met in Chapter 4) and Ivan Illich, to whom I now turn.

Schools don't do what they say they do

Ivan Illich was a key figure in bringing together thought about the purpose of school. In 1971, in his short book *Deschooling Society*, he made a powerful argument for getting rid of schools. In the first page of the book, he summarizes his message: 'the right to learn is curtailed by the obligation to attend school'.

He said that we confuse teaching with learning, grade advancement with education, a diploma with competence. He posed a challenge about learning: ask anyone to specify how they acquired what they know and value and they will very often, even those who reject progressive ideas, admit that they learned it outside school rather than within it. 'Their knowledge of facts, their understanding of life and work came to them from friendship or love, while viewing TV, or while reading, from examples of peers or the challenge of a street encounter' (p 75).

When I read this in the 1970s as I trained to be a teacher, it had a profound impact. What, indeed, had I learned from school that was remotely useful, I asked myself. There was some reading, writing, and arithmetic, I suppose, but my memories were of bad teaching that frightened me as a small child, to the extent that my parents, through teaching me themselves, had to sort out the problems that school was creating, for I was becoming scared of school and all that went with it. As I thought about the question, I had to accept that there was, in fact, very little that I could identify as actively beneficial to me in later life. The school experiences that had been useful, I reflected, were garnered incidentally—from friendships and from fights, from the occasional story from teachers as they departed from the syllabus, from meeting people I wouldn't otherwise have met, from incidental reading. As I thought about it, it seemed that Illich actually had a point.

Deschooling Society contains a chapter on learning webs. Reading it now, I find that Illich was strikingly prescient: 'The current search for new educational *funnels* [i.e. curricula, schools, and the 'hardware' of education] must be reversed into the search for their institutional inverse: education *webs* which heighten the opportunity for each one to transform each movement of his living into one of learning, sharing and caring.' He imagines networks of people getting together via central computers, exchanging contact details and information about their own skills or their own learning needs. 'It is amazing,' he continues, 'that such a simple

112

utility has never been used on a broad scale for publicly valued activity.' Remember that Illich was writing in the 1960s, long before anyone had heard very much about computers let alone thought about their potential for enhancing communication. He had seen social networking and its promise 30 years ahead of its actual appearance.

His extraordinary foresight extends to the ways that he conceptualizes failure to learn, seeing it as the consequence of poverty rather than learning difficulty or lack of intelligence. For more than a century educators have been all too ready to explain failure to learn through what are sometimes called 'within child' problems. The problem would be taken to be with what over the years would variously be called imbecility, educational subnormality, or, in today's soubriquet, learning difficulty. Or there would be a problem with the child's behaviour, called something such as maladjustment, emotional and behavioural difficulties, or ADHD (attention deficit hyperactivity disorder). (The labels change with time.) Illich's view, which was that school failure had more to do with a child's culture and school's inability to accommodate it than it had to do with inbuilt deficits, is the view many educators take today.

It is worth noting here that explanations based on children's deficits have shown extraordinary resilience, despite a steadily accumulating fund of knowledge which points to alternative explanations for failure. From studies of canal-boat children in the 1920s in Britain to studies of mountain children in the USA in the 1970s to today's work on geographical patterns of failure in US cities, the lesson is that it is cultural milieu rather than any psychological characteristic that determines a child's success or failure at school. Put simply, the explanation for school failure comes from poverty rather than 'difficulties' residing in the child, and Illich is surprisingly prescient in his recognition of this. His instinct was not to look toward the child for the cause of learning failure but toward school as an institution.

The interesting thing about Illich's analysis was not simply his dismissal of the traditional psychological and medical pseudo-explanations repeatedly offered by established education. It's interesting that he also rejected the kinds of solutions to learning failure which have come from more enlightened explanations of such failure. He looked at multi-billion-dollar programmes to support families living in poverty which aimed to enhance their children's educational performance. The evidence then, back in the sixties, from a programme called Title One, costing three billion dollars and providing compensatory education for six million children, was disappointing—as indeed it is from similar programmes implemented more recently.

His main point was that any school-based solution would inevitably be ineffective because the activities which go on in schools are too often not educational. Learning most often happens casually and for a purpose—that is to say a real purpose, not the purpose of pleasing the teacher or getting the right answer. Schools rarely enable casual learning, nor do they provide any real purpose for learning.

Despite their failure to deal with disadvantage, schools continued to haul toward them with tractor-beam-like power the major share of educational funds; they managed to do this because of the status always accorded to school as an institution and because of the huge vested interests devoted to their maintenance in more or less the same form. According to Illich, this pattern needed to be inverted. He said that 'there should be no obstacle for anyone at any time of his life to be able to choose instruction among hundreds of definable skills at public expense' (p 21). He envisaged 'edu-credit cards' which would be issued to people at birth and which would enable them to acquire the skills they needed 'at their convenience, better, faster, cheaper and with fewer undesirable side-effects than in school.'

You can see from this last statement that Illich wasn't against the learning of skills. Although he is sometimes portrayed as more of an insurgent than a teacher, more interested in revolution than education, it could be said that he was actually something of a conservative when it came to the purposes of education. Skills—the essence of teaching for formalists—were, for Illich too, a sine qua non of education; what he was against was the teaching of these skills *at school*. School was the problem. School, he asserted, because of its characteristics as an institution, failed to make learning meaningful.

Illich had admired the work of the Brazilian educator Paulo Freire, who provided for Illich something of a case study in the way that education should be conducted. Like John Locke and John Dewey, Freire saw education as an integral and necessary part of a healthy democracy: people had to understand their political situations for a society to be truly open and democratic. To this end, Freire had devoted his life to the education of his country's impoverished peasant population and through a process he described as *conscientização* sought to help his compatriots become literate while at the same time working for their freedom.

The literacy and the freedom weren't separate but, rather, inextricably connected. In his *Pedagogy of the Oppressed* he suggested that traditional forms of education served only to maintain the oppression of the poor. Literacy, he said, should not simply be used to 'improve' the peasants for the benefit of the people who were oppressing them: enhancing workers' literacy wasn't a way of producing better workers and more compliant consumers. Rather, education should help to elevate them, and help free them from oppression: it should be at the heart of the democratic process.

Freire got his hands dirty: he worked down among the people, and this is why his work has earned the admiration of so many across the world, in his combination of high ideals with nitty-gritty practice. His solutions to the issues he identified were not merely rhetorical or theoretical. He designed a highly practical scheme for teaching reading to illiterate adults based on words and phrases that were important to them in understanding their lives. In this sense, his work was consistent with the advice of Bruner and his spiral curriculum: start where the learner *is* and make it meaningful.

Freire seems to provide proof of Illich's point about the inappropriateness of school as an institution for education, for his out-of-school teaching programmes met with great success. A US Secretary for Health, Education, and Welfare, John Gardner, in 1965 made the controversial assertion that everything a high school graduate learns in twelve years of schooling could easily be learned in two years. Freire's adult learners, working outside the formal school environment and with a curriculum that was highly relevant for them, proved Gardner's point, as they acquired basic literacy in a matter of weeks. If this could be done, the wisdom of devoting several years of primary education to the same purpose—a project that often fails—was surely questionable. Here was evidence for Illich's argument that people learn best outside school.

What will the future bring?

For as long as I can remember, we have been on the threshold of a revolution in schooling. The critiques I have just reviewed together with the advances in access to knowledge brought by information technology combined to convince many people that school, as an institution, was dying. Indeed, I can clearly recall in 1985 a distinguished university dean giving an address in which he confidently (and rather pompously) predicted that schools would not exist at the turn of the millennium. Well, schools slipped through the turn of the millennium fully intact: indeed, they're in rude health—never been better—and there's no sign of any decline in their popularity. In fact, governments persist in providing more of the same: in 2015, the school leaving age in Britain will rise once more, this time to the age of eighteen years.

Why the shibboleth of continually rising school leaving ages and continually expanding higher education? Why not look hard at the 40 per cent who emerge from secondary school with very little, and ask why this is the case? Why do we force them to attend school when they don't want to attend and when there is so little evidence for the success of our certificate-orientated education system? Why not, from the age of fourteen onwards, offer Illich's edu-credit cards, which students would be able to use as they wish: apprenticeship, or staying on at school, or having the option of education later on—in their late teens, twenties, thirties, or beyond? Apart from anything else, it would be good to see schools normalized by the presence of a range of students of all ages.

In Burke and Grosvenor's *The School I'd Like*, Lorna, age fourteen, says this about the school she would like:

> I would like to see a weakening of the association of schools with children. Ideally, although I have some reservations as to the economical practicability, I would like to see an optional and comprehensive education system for all ages. This would help relationships between people of different generations, and give greater freedom to the young... The system should be flexible enough to allow people to specialise and follow their own interests and talents, and to catch up on other areas later on, if necessary.

Lorna, what excellent ideas! Where are you now? Some mixing in the age structure of schools wouldn't, indeed, go amiss, but we see little or no sign of any such radical restructuring mooted by governments.

We could look, too, at the other end of the education spectrum. Instead of feverishly striving to lower the point at which children start at school, why don't we look at the evidence and, instead, *raise* the age at which children start school, at the same time extending nursery education and programmes such as the UK's Sure Start, which provide families of young children with wide-ranging support and childcare? (Evaluation of Sure Start has shown that parents showed less negative parenting while providing their children with a better home learning environment.) Such an approach hasn't done the Finns any harm. In fact, as I've noted, their children have the best reading in the world. It's not hard to see why. None of us learns when we are pressured, frightened, or bored, and this is what happens to many children when they sense that the heat is on at school.

Or, if we are being guided by evidence, why not combine a couple of bits of significant evidence? Fact 1: we know that crude amount of time in school is less important than some people make out (children who spend large amounts of time in hospital, for example, don't seem to suffer much educationally). Fact 2: class size is important for quality of learning (actually, the evidence on this is complex, but I'm going with this, the common-sense interpretation of the evidence). Why not implement policy using these two facts to reduce numbers of children in school at any one time? Modularize more of the learning that happens at secondary school to accommodate greater flexibility in patterns of attendance and let those who aren't in school draw up a plan that describes what they will do with their time educationally outside school: network with other students on a project; go and work for a period; do community service; complete a library-based research project; plan an expedition; go on holiday with the grandparents; go on an exchange with a student in another country for a month; or whatever. Make it strange for young people to go to university at eighteen, and normal for them to go in their twenties or thirties after several years doing something else.

This brings us back to the point that I tried to make right at the beginning of the book: the words 'education' and 'schooling' are sometimes used interchangeably. Education, it is important to reassert here at the end of the book, is not the same as schooling. As Diane Ravitch, former adviser to the US government, put it after reviewing ten years of experience with President George

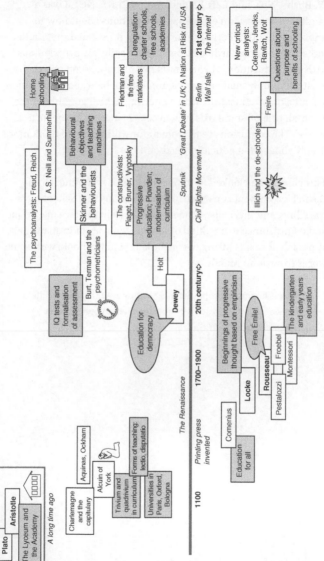

12. A (far from scale) timeline of education ideas

A long time ago

Plato
Aristotle
The Lyceum and the Academy

Charlemagne and the capitulary
Aquinas, Ockham
Alcuin of York
Trivium and quadrivium in curriculum
Forms of teaching: lectio, disputatio
Universities in Paris, Oxford, Bologna

The Renaissance

1100
Printing press invented
Comenius
Education for all

1700–1900
Beginnings of progressive thought based on empiricism
Locke
Rousseau
Free Émile!
Pestalozzi
Froebel
Montessori
The kindergarten and early years education

20th century
IQ tests and formalisation of assessment
Burt, Terman and the psychometricians
Education for democracy
Dewey
Holt
Progressive education: Plowden; modernisation of curriculum
The constructivists: Piaget, Bruner, Vygotsky
Skinner and the behaviourists
Behavioural objectives and teaching machines
The psychoanalysts: Freud, Reich
A.S. Neill and Summerhill
Home schooling
Friedman and the free marketeers

Sputnik

Civil Rights Movement

'Great Debate' in UK; A Nation at Risk in USA

Berlin Wall falls

Deregulation: charter schools, free schools, academies

21st century
The internet

Illich and the de-schoolers
Freire
New critical analysts: Coleman, Jencks, Ravitch, Wolf
Questions about purpose and benefits of schooling

W. Bush's 'No Child Left Behind' Act (NCLB): 'NCLB was a punitive law based on erroneous assumptions about how to improve schools… Perhaps most naively, it assumed that higher test scores on standardized tests of basic skills are synonymous with good education.' Ravitch puts her finger here on one of the most commonly made mistakes in public debate about education: a confusion of 'education' with something which goes under the catch-all title of 'standards', which seems, in turn, to mean 'test scores'. The confusion stems from an unwillingness to think more deeply about what education is about.

This chapter has looked at some critiques of schooling. Given Ravitch's comments on some of the directions that schooling is travelling, and given also school's resilience in the face of critique and its resistance to any kind of serious innovation in shape or approach, it seems fitting to conclude it, and the book, with some words from John Marsh:

> If schools do not disproportionately improve—or harm—the life chances of their charges… why not free them to pursue other educational ends? (p 206)

References and further reading

Chapter 1: Beginnings

Bowles, S. and Gintis, H. (1999) *Schooling in capitalist America: educational reform and the contradictions of economic life.* New York: Basic Books.

Harleian Miscellany (1810) A collection of scarce, curious, and entertaining pamphlets and tracts, as well in manuscript as in print; found in the late Earl of Oxford's library, interspersed with historical, political, and critical notes. London: Robert Dutton.

Leach, A.F. (1915) *The schools of medieval England.* London: Methuen & Co. Ltd (this can be found in the excellent online 'The history of education in England').

Plato (2007) *The Republic.* London: Penguin.

Postman, N. (1994) *The disappearance of childhood.* New York: Vintage Books.

Rousseau, J.-J. ([1762]1993) *Émile* (trans. B. Foxley). London: J.M. Dent.

Trevelyan, G.M. (1978) *English social history: a survey of six centuries from Chaucer to Queen Victoria.* London: Longman.

- For a discussion of the growth of childhood as an idea, see Ariès, P. (1962) *Centuries of childhood* (trans. Robert Baldrick). New York: Vintage Books. It is interesting to see how the school grows in tandem with this development.
- Good for a discussion of Aristotle is Ackrill, J.L. (1988) *A new Aristotle reader* (Princeton: Princeton University Press). For education, see especially the chapter on politics (Chapter VIII).

- Pearson, L.E. (1967) *Elizabethans at home* (Stanford: Stanford University Press) gives a very readable account of how education developed in late Tudor England.

Chapter 2: Oil and water: the formal and the progressive

Aristotle (1962) *The politics* (trans. T.A. Sinclair). London: Penguin.

Cockburn, J.S., King, H.P.F. and McDonnell, K.G.T. (eds) (1969) *A History of the County of Middlesex*: Vol 1, pp 255–85. Available at: http://www.british-history.ac.uk/report.aspx?compid=22125 (accessed 14 August 2011).

Dewey, J. (1938) *Experience and education*. New York: Collier Books.

Locke, J. ([1693] 1996) *Some thoughts concerning education and Of the conduct of understanding* (with an introduction by R.W. Grant and N. Tarcov). Indianapolis: Hackett Publishing Co. Inc.

- For a view of Rousseau which incorporates discussion of his fascinating life, look at Wokler, R. (2001) *Rousseau: a very short introduction* (Oxford: Oxford University Press).
- An excellent, readable discussion of Dewey and Oakeshott (and the meanings and purposes of education) can be found in Pring, R. (2004) *Philosophy of educational research* (London: Continuum).
- An excellent source on progressive and informal education is *Infed* at http://www.infed.org/

Chapter 3: The traditions unfold: ideas into practice

Alexander, R.J. (2001) *Culture and pedagogy: international comparisons in primary education*. London: Wiley-Blackwell.

Bennett, N. (1976) *Teaching styles and pupil progress*. London: Open Books.

Burke, C. and Grosvenor, I. (2003) *The school I'd like: children and young people's reflections on an education for the 21st century*. London: Routledge.

- A good discussion of contemporary thinking about progressive ideas in use in the classroom can be found in Brown, A.L. and

Campione, J.C. (1990) Communities of learning and thinking, or a context by any other name, in D. Kuhn *Developmental perspectives on teaching and learning skills*, Vol 21, pp 108–26 (Basel: Karger).

- International comparison data is usually obtained through the OECD's Programme for International Student Assessment (PISA), Trends in International Mathematics and Science Study (TIMSS), and Progress in International Reading Literacy Study (PIRLS). For the statistics used in the text I have drawn from these:

  ○ OECD/UNESCO-UIS (2003) Literacy skills for the world of tomorrow. Retrieved from http://www.pisa.oecd.org/dataoecd/43/9/33690591.pdf

  ○ OECD (2010) PISA 2009 results: Executive summary. Retrieved from http://www.pisa.oecd.org/dataoecd/54/12/46643496.pdf

- Further information on the comparisons of curricula I mention can be gained from the write-up of the major evaluation of Follow Through: Schweinhart, L.J. and Weikart, D.P. (1997) Lasting differences: the HighScope preschool curriculum comparison through age 23, *Early Childhood Research Quarterly*, 12, 117–43.

- The original discussion of the ecology of the classroom can be found in Walter Doyle's classic article: Doyle, W. (1977) The uses of non-verbal behaviours: toward an ecological view of classrooms, *Merrill-Palmer Quarterly*, 23, 3, 179–92.

- You can find Project ORACLE described in full detail in Galton, M.J., Simon, B. and Croll, P. (1980) *Inside the primary classroom* (London: Routledge and Kegan Paul). With other colleagues, Galton later wrote *Inside the primary classroom: twenty years on*, which gives a good account of changes in education over that period.

- A comprehensive American take on reform can be found in Tyack, D. and Cuban, L. (1995) *Tinkering toward utopia: a century of public school reform* (Cambridge, MA: Harvard University Press).

- A rebuttal of the claim about rising standards on the basis of top-down 'guidance' from government can be found in Tymms, P.

(2004) Are standards rising in English primary schools, *British Educational Research Journal*, 30, 4, 477–94.

- I discuss the Finnish approach to education (by contrast with the idea in the English-speaking world that teachers ought to be directed to use this or that method) in Thomas, G. (2012) Changing our landscape of inquiry for a new science of education, *Harvard Educational Review*, 82, 1, 26–51.

Chapter 4: Big ideas from the 20th century

Ball, S. (2008) *The education debate*. Bristol: The Policy Press.

Burke, C. and Grosvenor, I. (2003) *The school I'd like: children and young people's reflections on an education for the 21st century*. London: Routledge.

Claxton, G. (2008) *What's the point of school?* Oxford: Oneworld Publications.

Cox, C.E. and Dyson, A.E. (1971) *The Black Papers on education*. London: Davis-Poynter.

Cremin, L. (1961) *The transformation of the school: progressivism in American education 1876–1957*. New York: Knopf.

Dewey, J. (1916) *Democracy and education*. New York: Free Press.

Dewey, J. (1963) *Experience and education*. New York: Collier Books (originally published in 1938 by Kappa Delta Pi).

Hadow Report (1931) The Board of Education's Report of the Consultative Committee on the Primary School. Available at http://www.educationengland.org.uk/documents/hadow1931/3100.html

Holt, J. (1964) *How children fail*. New York: Pitman Publishing Company.

Kilpatrick, W.H. (1918) The project method, *Teachers College Record*, 19, 319–35.

Minow, M. (2010) *In Brown's wake: legacies of America's educational landmark*. New York: Oxford University Press.

Plowden Report (1967) Children and their primary schools. Available at http://www.educationengland.org.uk/documents/plowden/

Postman, N. and Weingartner, C. (1971) *Teaching as a subversive activity*. London: Penguin.

Ravitch, D. (2010) *The death and life of the great American school system: how testing and choice are undermining education*. New York: Basic Books.

Sandel, M. (2012) *What money can't buy: the moral limits of the market*. London: Allen Lane.

U.S. Supreme Court (1954) *Brown et al. v. Board of Education of Topeka et al.* appeal from the United States District Court for the District of Kansas, 347 U.S. 483.

- Friedman's essay on vouchers is: Friedman, M. (1955) The role of government in education, in R.A. Solo (ed.) *Economics and the Public Interest* (Chapel Hill, NC: Rutgers University Press).
- Further discussion on Plowden can be found in the journal *FORUM*, which in 2007 had two issues on Plowden forty years on (Vol 49, Numbers 1 & 2).
- An excellent coverage on education in the marketplace is available from Bridges, D. and Jonathan, R. (2003) Education and the market, in N. Blake, P. Smeyers, R. Smith and P. Standish (eds) *The Blackwell guide to the philosophy of education* (Oxford: Blackwell).
- A highly readable analysis of the application of market ideology to public services is in Seddon, J. (2008) *Systems thinking in the public sector* (Axminster: Triarchy Press).
- To see the escorting of James Meredith onto Mississippi University campus, ask YouTube to find you 'James Meredith University of Mississippi 1962 Integration Riot Newsreel'.
- I look at the story of segregation in special education in Thomas, G. (2013) A review of thinking and research about inclusive education policy, with suggestions for a new kind of inclusive thinking, *British Educational Research Journal*, 39(3).
- John Claughton's full comments on the DNA of private schools and selection can be found in the summer edition of the online magazine *Attain*, available at http://www.attainmagazine.co.uk/politics/a-reply-to-lord-adonis/

Chapter 5: Analysts and theorists: what did they ever do for us?

Bernstein, B. (1973) *Class, codes and control: theoretical studies towards a sociology of language*. London: HarperCollins.

Bryant, P.E. (1984). Piaget, teachers and psychologists. *Oxford Review of Education*, 10(3), 251–9.

Crowther Report (1959) 15 to 18. Available at http://www.educationengland.org.uk/documents/crowther/

Fienberg, S.E. and Resnick, D.P. (1997) Re-examining *The bell curve*, in B. Devlin, S.E. Fienberg, D.P. Resnick and K. Roeder (eds) *Intelligence, genes and success: scientists respond to* The bell curve. New York, NY: Springer-Verlag.

Herrnstein, R.J. and Murray, C. (1994) *The bell curve: intelligence and class structure in American life*. New York, NY: The Free Press.

Jensen, A. (1969) How much can we boost IQ and scholastic achievement? *Harvard Educational Review*, 39(1): 123.

Lippmann, W. (1922) The mental age of Americans, *The New Republic*, 25 October. 213–15.

Marmot, M. (2010) Fair society, healthy lives: the Marmot review—strategic review of health inequalities in England post-2010. London: UCL. Available at: www.ucl.ac.uk/marmotreview (accessed 28 February 2011).

Reimer, E. (1971) *School is dead*. London: Penguin.

Terman, L.M. (1924) The possibilities and limitations of training, *Journal of Educational Research*, 10: 335–43.

Vygotsky, L.S. (1978) *Mind in society: development of higher psychological processes*. Boston: Harvard University Press.

Willms, J.D. (1999) Quality and inequality in children's literacy: the effects of families, schools and communities, in D. Keating and C. Hertzman (eds) *Developmental health and the wealth of nations: social, biological, and educational dynamics* (New York, Guilford Press) (pp 72–94).

- Burt's fraud and the evidence for it are discussed by Hearnshaw, L.S. (1979) *Cyril Burt: psychologist* (London: Hodder and Stoughton) and Kamin, L.J. (1977) Burt's IQ data, *Science*, 195: 246–8.

- For specific discussion of Piaget and conservation, see Elkind, D. (1967) Piaget's conservation problems, *Child Development*, 38, 15–27.

- For an excellent and easy-to-follow summary of recent issues to do with education and social justice, see Smith, E. (2012) *Key issues in education and social justice* (London: Sage). (It's written for undergraduate students.)

- The Sutton Trust's website gives excellent analyses of access to higher education.

Chapter 6: The curriculum

Bruner, J. (1977) *The process of education*. Cambridge, MA: Harvard University Press.

Cannadine, D., Keating, J. and Sheldon, N. (2011) *The right kind of history*. Basingstoke: Palgrave.

Jackson, P. (1968) *Life in classrooms*. New York: Holt, Rinehart and Winston.

Marshall, H.E. (2007) *Our island story: a history of Britain for boys and girls from the Romans to Queen Victoria*. London: Civitas.

Peddiwell, J.A. (1939) *The saber-tooth curriculum*. New York: McGraw-Hill.

Postman, N. (1996) *The end of education*. New York: Alfred A. Knopf.

Reimer, E. (1971) *School is dead*. London: Penguin.

Stenhouse, L. (1975) *An introduction to curriculum research and development*. London: Heinemann. Also see Rudduck, J. and Hopkins, D. (eds) (1985) *Research as a basis for teaching: readings from the work of Lawrence Stenhouse*. London: Heinemann.

Whitehead, A.N. (1929) *The aims of education and other essays*. London: Macmillan.

Wragg, E.C. (1997) *The cubic curriculum*. London: Routledge.

- For an extended discussion of Bruner's spiral curriculum, try Alexander, R. (2008) *Essays on pedagogy* (London: Routledge). See especially Chapter 7.
- For a discussion of transfer of training, and the chess example, see Klein, P. (1997) Multiplying the problems of intelligence by eight: a critique of Gardner's theory, *Canadian Journal of Education*, 22(4): 377–94.

Chapter 7: School's out!

Burke, C. and Grosvenor, I. (2003) *The school I'd like: children and young people's reflections on an education for the 21st century*. London: Routledge.

Freire, P. (1970) *Pedagogy of the oppressed*. London: Penguin.

Illich, I. (1973) *Deschooling society*. London: Penguin.

Jencks, C. et al. (1973) *Inequality: a reassessment of the effect of family and schooling in America*. London: Allen Lane.

Marsh, J. (2011) *Class dismissed: why we cannot teach or learn our way out of inequality*. New York: Monthly Review Press.

Minow, M. (2010) *In Brown's wake: legacies of America's educational landmark*. New York: Oxford University Press, USA.

Ravitch, D. (2000). *Left back: a century of failed school reforms*. New York: Simon & Schuster.

Wolf, A. (2002) *Does education matter? Myths about education and economic growth*. London: Penguin Books.

- Sir Ken Robinson beautifully sums up some of today's misconceptions about schooling in his clip on YouTube: 'RSA animate—changing education paradigms'. He also entertainingly debunks the ADHD 'epidemic'.

- Statistics such as those on the growth in the numbers of degrees awarded can be obtained online from the National Center for Education Statistics for the USA, and the Department for Education Research and Statistics Gateway for the UK.

- Summerhill, Neill's philosophy, and the recent battles with the inspectorate are covered well in Vaughan, M. (2006) *Summerhill and A.S. Neill* (Maidenhead: Open University Press).

- Early home education is discussed interestingly in Musgrove, F. (1972) Middle-class families and schools, 1780–1880, in P.W. Musgrave *Sociology, history and education* (London: Methuen).

- Ronald Dore looks at how education has come to mean simply the earning of qualifications. He focuses especially on the educational histories of Britain, Japan, Sri Lanka, and Kenya: Dore, R. (1997) *The diploma disease* (London: Institute of Education).

- If you are interested in comparing early and contemporary discussions of the relationship of culture to education, look at:
  - Gordon, H. (1923) Mental and scholastic tests among retarded children. Education Pamphlet 44. London: HMSO.
  - Wheeler, L.R. (1970) A trans-decade comparison of the IQs of Tennessee mountain children, in I. Al-Issa and W. Dennis

(eds) *Cross-cultural studies of behavior* (New York: Holt, Rinehart and Winston) (pp 120–33).

○ Artiles, A. J. (2003) Special education's changing identity: paradoxes and dilemmas in views of culture and space, *Harvard Educational Review*, 73, 164–202.

• For the Sure Start evaluation, see *The impact of Sure Start local programmes on three year olds and their families* at http://www.ness.bbk.ac.uk/impact/documents/42.pdf

Index

SOCIAL MEDIA
Very Short Introduction

Join our community
www.oup.com/vsi

- Join us online at the official Very Short Introductions
  Facebook page.
- Access the thoughts and musings of our authors with our
  online **blog**.
- Sign up for our monthly **e-newsletter** to receive information
  on all new titles publishing that month.
- Browse the full range of Very Short Introductions online.
- Read **extracts** from the Introductions for free.
- Visit our library of **Reading Guides**. These guides, written by our
  expert authors will help you to question again, why you think
  what you think.
- If you are a teacher or lecturer you can order inspection
  copies quickly and simply via our website.

Visit the Very Short Introductions website to access all this and
more for free.
www.oup.com/vsi

ORGANIZATIONS
A Very Short Introduction
Mary Jo Hatch

This *Very Short Introductions* addresses all of these questions and considers many more. Mary Jo Hatch introduces the concept of organizations by presenting definitions and ideas drawn from the a variety of subject areas including the physical sciences, economics, sociology, psychology, anthropology, literature, and the visual and performing arts. Drawing on examples from prehistory and everyday life, from the animal kingdom as well as from business, government, and other formal organizations, Hatch provides a lively and thought provoking introduction to the process of organization.

Expand your collection of
VERY SHORT INTRODUCTIONS